To. James, Stephen and Susan

Frontispiece. Gouche/watercolour painting of the back of the Frome Bridge by David Grapes.

Onto The Bridge

by

Geoff Swaine

TRAFFORD

By the Same Author
Up The Line Crowood Press 2000

Note for Librarians: A cataloguing record for this book is available from Library and Archives Canada at www.collectionscanada.ca/amicus/index-e.html
ISBN 1-4120-2933-3

green power

Printed in Victoria, BC, Canada. Printed on paper with minimum 30% recycled fibre. Trafford's print shop runs on "green energy" from solar, wind and other environmentally-friendly power sources.

TRAFFORD
PUBLISHING™
Offices in Canada, USA, Ireland and UK
This book was published *on-demand* in cooperation with Trafford Publishing. On-demand publishing is a unique process and service of making a book available for retail sale to the public taking advantage of on-demand manufacturing and Internet marketing. On-demand publishing includes promotions, retail sales, manufacturing, order fulfilment, accounting and collecting royalties on behalf of the author.

Book sales for North America and international:
Trafford Publishing, 6E–2333 Government St.,
Victoria, BC v8t 4p4 CANADA
phone 250 383 6864 (toll-free 1 888 232 4444)
fax 250 383 6804; email to orders@trafford.com
Book sales in Europe:
Trafford Publishing (uk) Limited, 9 Park End Street, 2nd Floor
Oxford, UK ox1 1hh UNITED KINGDOM
phone 44 (0)1865 722 113 (local rate 0845 230 9601)
facsimile 44 (0)1865 722 868; info.uk@trafford.com
Order online at:
trafford.com/04-0761

10 9 8 7 6 5 4

Contents

PART ONE   Evacuated to Frome   13
    (My days in the Market Town)

PART TWO   Notes from my father   73
    (His young life in Frome)

PART THREE   Development of the Woollen Industry   115
    (From the early days to the 1800s in Frome)

PART FOUR   Researching the Past   141
    (1837 to 1936)

Introduction

The Bridge in Frome is a unique structure. It has buildings on one side consisting of 3 storey houses and integral shops, and continues to fascinate visitors and residents of the town. The present bridge, which was built in 1821, replaced an earlier structure, which dated from 1667.

The Swaine family had a tailoring business in the middle of the terrace on the bridge for almost a hundred years, and they also had the adjoining house and shop, which sold ladies hats and accessories.

This book tells the story of the life surrounding numbers 5 & 6 The Bridge during and beyond the days of the business. My days were from the forties to the sixties, and my father gives his recollections of his boyhood days in the 1920's. The town has a long history of being involved in the woollen industry and a section is also added to try and trace the workings of this industry back to its origins. Also an attempt is made to give some history pointers about the growth of the town and its incorporation as a market town. A final section is about my family history searches and the different families of the town which have crossed with the Swaine's. This search was quite revealing and pulled together much information that had previously been lost to the family.

Swaine's appear in different registers around north and east Somerset going back to the 1600's, in places such as Wells and Bruton. The ongoing records link up to the present with sometimes the name spelt differently i.e. Swayne or Swain. Registration and documentation were sparse before 1840 when, in that year, proper documentation began. Previously the clergyman of the Parish may have made the only recording of a birth. He would often write the name down just as he heard it.

As time goes by it is becoming easier to trace family history records. This is because all the records are being centralised on library microfiche and County Hall computers. The Internet now is also well advanced with Family Tree sites.

Frome had been a wool-town for many centuries with the earliest record of wool being noted in the twelfth century. Since the sixteenth century wealthy industrialists had become involved, and by the late 1700's Frome's woollen industry became mechanised by water-power. It was then well caught up in the Industrial Revolution, when the industry was at its height.

Slumps in work happened at various times along the way just as they do now. This leads to migrations of workers from one area to another in the search for work. A major slump occurred in the early nineteenth century when Frome lost nearly all of its cloth business.

There was migration of workers away from the area, which probably included some of my ancestors. Many folk left for Yorkshire, and perhaps in earlier times there had been migration the other way. There was just one Swaine family to remain in the town, and they were to start the tailoring business.

The Swaine name had been prominent with woollen people around the Bradford area, and we suspect that some of them have origins in the Frome area. The biggest cluster of Swaine's in Britain is now in West Yorkshire with over fifty households registered.

The tailoring firm of W. Swaine and Son began in Frome in 1837. Firstly at Catherine Hill, and then from 1841, they had moved to No.6 The Bridge.

A two-storey timber structure built on stilts shows up on many old photographs of the back of the bridge, this was built later to expand the business. This structure was to house the employees, with lower floor for girl machinists, and the upper floor being the tailoring room where men worked.

My Grandfather was the last incumbent of the business before it got caught up in the depressed times of the 1930's and closed.

Grandfather was a very keen gardener, and for a long time he had a garden on an island site just behind Singers factory, along from the bridge. He would go along to there by rowing boat from the landing stage at the back. The business finally closed in 1936; the end of the business and sale of the property is part of this story.

My father, Bill Swaine was born at Catherine Hill House in Frome in 1913, and he had an elder sister Mary who was born three years before.

Bill went to school at Sexey's School in Bruton as a day boarder. His aspirations were very much as an academic, and so he was never going to be a candidate for the tailoring business. In 1929 he left Frome to go and work in the City of London. It was there he met my mother and they made their life in London.

The property next door to the tailoring business, No.5 The Bridge, in later years was owned by my grandfather's sister (my great aunt) Helen Neale.

This is where grandfather spent his last years, and is the home of my memories. Aunt ran the shop right through to 1956 when she was in her 80's. Kelly's Directory shows that in 1889, this shop was run by (Misses) Agnes & Ellen Swaine, as a Berlin wool and fancy repository, so it had also been in the family for a long time.

Frome in the fifties was a busy market town. The population of about 12,000 people were, as typical of the times, dependant on public transport. Western National ran the bus service to Trowbridge, with the Bristol Company running most of the other services.

Crown Tours were the long-standing local coach company to take people on leisure trips. Many a trip did we make with them. From time to time a long distance Royal Blue coach would pass through to take passengers along the A4 to London. Stopping outside the Crown Hotel, it was unknowingly following the old mail-coach runs of the past.

The railways well served the town with a loop coming off the main line into Frome Station. The Frome to Bristol branch line was a very typical sleepy line, but in the end it was under used and closed for passenger traffic in 1958. For many years in later life my grandfather had his garden beside the line at Garston Farm. There was a watercress bed beside the line near North Parade, which always served him well too.

After the tailoring business closed in 1936. My grandfather and grandmother took a tenancy at Conigre House, the big Regency style house close to Singers Factory. It is there that I have my earliest memories of life, with its big garden and Mulberry tree.

I was born in 1942 in Maidenhead, where Dad was stationed with the RAF. Soon afterwards my mother had to move us on, but it was too dangerous to take us back to her folks in London, so we were evacuated to Frome and Conigre House. It was there we stayed for most of the war before moving in with Aunt at 5 The Bridge.

I went to nursery at Rook Lane Church and then to the infant school at Christchurch Street. It was only a short schooling because it was to be soon, Spring 1947 in fact, that we moved back to London, to a house on the Duke of Bedford's Estate in Bloomsbury Square.

A while later Grandmother became ill and finally passed away in 1950. Grandfather then gave up Conigre House, and moved back onto The Bridge to live with his sister.

The present town bridge continues to be one of the main attractions of the town. The terrace of houses with shops that line the east side of the bridge is like no other.

Nowadays estate agents, an Indian Restaurant and other enterprises, which represent the commerce of today, occupy the properties. In the past it was different, but just about everything else was too.

The rapid advances made during the last forty years of the twentieth century have changed everything. Life before was so much different, back in the sleepy fifties. This was the last decade when old values and habits prevailed. Frome had only changed gradually over the centuries and things were slow and dignified. My early experiences in life were in those times, and this book is in appreciation of that.

PART ONE

one

I ride up the winding Clink Road, my newly obtained bike giving me a freedom I never had before. Leaving behind Badgers Hill and the football ground, the farmyard smells are very prominent. Pedalling fast, this road that had once been so long now seemed quite short. Ahead is my favourite spot, only matched by Platform 10 at Kings Cross Station in London, but that is my other life, I am now down in Frome, a little market town in Somerset, for my twice yearly school holiday, this time for 6 weeks.

Arriving at the railway bridge, and quickly getting off the bike, I hitch myself up the parapet of the bridge. With my hands taking in the weathered stone I am checking the situation below. All is quiet. Still out of breath from the ride, it's nice just to take in the location, and breath the fresh air.

Moving off the bridge, I am through the wire fence and sitting on the embankment of the old Great Western Railway main line. Diagonally opposite is the signal box, and just beyond that are the points, with the curve of the line going in towards Frome.

All is still quiet and there is hardly a house within a mile. A rare car passes over the bridge and provides a passing sound. The grasshoppers make their little noises, and birds are singing somewhere.

The telegraph wires add perspective. Supported high in the air they loop from pole to pole falling into the distance for half a mile down the line ahead

I am taking in the peace and tranquillity, when a bell rings in the signal box. The signalman is up and answering the code with taps on his machine. Another bell rings and he starts pulling the levers in front of him. The wires that run beside the line are straining, I wonder which signal is going to fall. It is the danger signal on the fast line from the west. Up the line more signals move as he pulls different levers. Then silence.

From the west a slight noise can be heard, a train is approaching. It comes around the Rodden bend and is moving very quickly. Racing forward and with the sound increasing, I hear the front bogie wheels hitting every joint in the track. Over the points it thunders and races past me. I get the number and name of the engine. It may be a King, or a Castle, or perhaps a County. All great locomotives designed in the same classical style.

The train was gone, and unexpectedly another train had crept up on the westbound line and was being held at the bridge signal. The signalman moves the points, drops the signal indicating 'Into Frome,' and the train whistles and moves brightly forward. I check the engine, this time it is a Hall, the great workhorses of the region. It has a very mysterious name, Dumbleton Hall; I wonder where that might be. On the side of the carriages is a long destination board, which reads - Paddington, Westbury, Frome, Castle Cary, Weymouth. This is the train I was on a few days ago, it would have changed engines at Westbury. Gathering speed it takes the curve off points, and I watch the taillight disappear.

It is suddenly quiet again, I notice the breeze now making a whistling sound as it passes through the telegraph wires. The signalman goes back to his newspaper or pools coupon. His day is a solitary 8-hour shift. Soon I will have to ride off home, I know the time by the trains that run past. The Cornish Riviera Express races west at about 12-20, Grandad will not tolerate me being late for dinner. It is at 1 o'clock sharp, not a minute sooner or a minute later. I will speed down those hills. I might later be going out with him.

I am only eleven years of age, and am sure life will always be like this, it always has been so why should it change.

Wait a minute, by George! I have just snapped out of my daydream. It is nearly half a century later and I am in a cold sweat. My head is in my hands, and my elbows are hurting on the desk.

Could my favourite place still be like that? Of course not, there haven't been steam engines since 1968. I went there a little while ago to check it out.

Oh dear, the signal box is gone, but that is to be expected. All signalling for miles is controlled from Westbury. Electric lights have replaced all the arm signals. A train goes by but I don't hear any click clicking of the wheels, all the rails are welded together, the train looks very clinical and efficient. I moved to the bank and, oh dear! They have built houses right up to the edge of the slope where the signal box used to be. There goes the solitude. This housing has been permitted because both Bath and Bristol have been over-developed and now they have picked on Frome to take the expansion. I was shocked that it had crept this far,

Oh, by the way, the stone bridge has gone, replaced by a wider concrete structure to take more traffic. There is not much left of the old embankment that I used to sit on. A big 4-lane dual-carriageway road has been built parallel to the railway not 20 yards behind. I can now hear the drone of constant traffic.

Nothing is the same.

So, what was Frome like all those years ago in the sleepy 1950's? It was the last great decade of the steam engine, although I didn't know it at the time. I couldn't bear to watch the decline in the sixties, with those beautiful machines being scrapped. Also, the fifties was the last decade where Victorian values prevailed, and Britain's industry was still intact. It was before motorways, yellow lines, television (for most), and very few families had cars. It was the time when I was growing up.

For my version of events, I begin in 1945 when I was three.

Life takes you on a great journey,
But travel backwards, and there is no mercy.

two

My earliest recollections of life are in the garden of Conigre House in Frome. The large Regency style house just beyond the Singers Factory, and a good result that was too, I had no complaints about where life had placed me.

The large house was a warren, and to explore it was a game in itself. Outside there was the big lawned garden with a wooded area at the side to be lost in, and there was a chicken run to the other side with workshops at the back of the house.

Me being the only grandson, I was a novelty. Two girls had come along before, they were my sister Jill, and cousin Sue and so I was something new. I was to be there for my early years, and my grand-parents would laugh at my antics and remarks. I played up to them quite willingly.

Grandchildren had appeared late in life for them, for they were both in their sixties. Long gone were the shackles of the family business, life for them now was for enjoyment. I would be running around the garden and getting into everything, while Jill would be sitting thoughtfully on the swing below the broken down Mulberry tree.

The Swaine family tailoring business had operated at No.6 The Bridge for nearly a hundred years, and had been wound up in 1936. Its last years had been a struggle in a depressed Frome, it was also a time when the multiple shops such as Burtons and the Co-op had moved in, the days of so many small traders were coming to an end. The Westminster Bank had forced their hand to close the business and the property was sold. The family though, came out of it quite well, and there was a little money left over afterwards.

The adjoining property No.5 The Bridge was still in the family, and was occupied by my great aunt. She had always run a hat shop there, from the turn of the century.

It was long before the winding up of the tailoring business when my father had moved to London, life for him was not to be in a small town, he pursued a career in the City of London. There he spent his early adult years and had met my mother. They had married and set up home. Life had seemed well set for them, until that is, there was the little matter of world war two being declared.

By 1942, Dad had been posted to Bracknell in Berkshire with the RAF, and they lived in accommodation in Maidenhead. Soon after this, they were to be delighted by the birth of their second child, me.

After I had arrived, the decision was made to dispatch us to Frome. Space in Maidenhead was limited, and going back to London was not an option. There were buzz bombs and V2 rockets about to be dropped out of the sky. Mother had taken us back their briefly, but it was too dangerous. Dad was to remain with the war effort, but for us it was evacuation. We would be going to Frome and Dad would only be able to see us when weekend passes permitted.

Evacuated to Frome as a baby, this was the life and place that I would get to know, and once out of the confines of Conigre House life was seen from a pram and pushchair. The little wrought iron lamppost that was on the first corner out of the house was an early landmark. It is no wonder that I was always fond of them.

Soon I was growing up fast, it was not long before I was following my grandfather everywhere. I was to have a very close relationship with him that lasted right through to 1962, a stern forthright man moulded from the days of the past.

He had a second garden on an island site down by the river at a place they called Waterloo, and sometimes I got taken down there. A lush water meadow with a wooden footbridge to be crossed to get to it, there was a platform on the other side for mooring a rowing boat. This was his little retreat, an idyllic little haven where the world stood still. It was always his garden from the days when they lived above the tailoring business on The Bridge. He had then rowed a boat down to it from the landing stage underneath the timber workshop. The island was almost totally secluded and he had made a garden among all the apple trees and fruit bushes.

Back at the house all the tools in the workshop fascinated me. Wooden planes, spoke-shaves, screwdrivers, and even a fretwork machine. There was what seemed like hundreds of other little chisels, drills and the suchlike, and they all had one thing in common - all the metal was black.

Grandad had largely furnished the big house with furniture bought from salerooms, a big selection there was too, all bought for a song. The house was full to the hilt with what today would be highly sought after pieces. There was one item that Jill and I were quite appreciative of, and that was a bed warming pan on a long pole. Grandad would put hot coal in it from the fire, and then slide the pan up and down in our beds before we got in. Very comforting it was too in the winter when there was ice on both sides of the bedroom window.

During 1943, Mother had had an accident when a branch of a tree fell and hit her. She was taken into Victoria Hospital for a while, and then needed a period of convalescence. Fortunately the grandparents were on hand to look after us.

Our stay in Frome was to last right through to the spring of 1947, but not all of that time was spent at Conigre House. Between the time that the war ended and our return to London, we had moved to stay with my great aunt at No. 5 The Bridge, it seemed that we had outstayed our welcome with my grandparents.

My great aunt was affectionately known as Aunt Peale, she had run her hat shop there since before the First World War. A very kindly lady who couldn't do enough for our family. She had willingly taken us in, and my younger sister Angela was born soon after this. I think that mum was more comfortable there and would feel less intimidated. Aunt was always on hand to take Angela out in her pram, with mum looking after the house and doing the cooking.

I attended the nursery at Rook Lane Chapel for a little while and remember that well. I was obviously none too impressed about the place, because on one occasion I ran off home. They had tried to make us sleep every afternoon on mats, and probably that was the last thing that I wanted to do. A young woman came looking for me. I expect that she was a bit distraught, but I was found at the back of the shop. She carried me back up to the nursery via Cheap Street and the Church steps. I don't think that I lasted there much longer after that. I did attend the little infant school in Christchurch Street before we came back to London, mum would take me, and we would each walk up one of the lines of cobblestones in Gentle Street.

three

Moving back to London 1947-1950

I had not knowingly been to London before we moved back there in the spring of 1947, and a cultural shock it was to be. My first memory after arriving at Paddington Station was seeing a bus with a white spot on the back. This had remained from the days of the blackouts, and so much else of the surroundings gave grim reminders of the war and the aftermath.

Mum, Dad and us three children were to live in one of the Duke of Bedford's properties in Bloomsbury Square. These smart houses had been requisitioned by the Council due to the gross shortage of housing after the bombing. (Mum and Dads previous London flat in Tavistock Place had been bombed, so they were on the Holborn housing list).

The whole area had received massive bombing, and the Theobalds Road area, where I was to attend school, was almost completely flattened. This was now a couple of years after the war and all the rubble had been cleared away, most of the bombsites had been levelled off with low walls built around them.

It was not long before I was getting used to seeing and playing on these wastelands. Generally they were safe, although a few fragile skeletons of buildings were still standing in places; these were distinctly dangerous.

I was placed into St George the Martyr infant School, which was near Queen Square. On one side were the hospitals of Gt.Ormond Street and on the other – nothing, that is except these bombsites.

After a very short time I realised that I was not very struck with this place. But, as children have absolutely no say in where they live, life had to go on. The family lived in the cramped top floor of the house, and things were tense. I was difficult, I do know that and didn't want to be there. For the next couple of years there were to be different degrees of turmoil. It was the post war austerity period and food and sweets were rationed, and life was generally tough.

There were two things though that were to change my life for the better. Dad had become a season ticket holder at the Arsenal Football Club and took me along to see a reserve team game, and the other was that our house was within a mile or two of all of the big London railway stations, and I liked trains.

Dad loved travelling around London, and soon I was going everywhere with him, the places also fascinated me, we would take in bus, train, tram or trolley bus rides. The trams lasted in London until 1951, and often we would go to football in these noisy contraptions, trolley buses lasted a little longer. Both came down Theobalds Road, with the trams going on down the Kingsway tunnel to emerge again at the Embankment, while the trolley buses turned around at Red Lion Square.

More and more would we go to Arsenal reserve games, and this would not only be to home games at Highbury, we would be off to all the other grounds where the team would be playing. Other times we would be going off to places like Epsom Downs, or Potters Bar watching the steam express trains fly along, or to any other place that took his fancy.

During this period the family would have short holidays at Frome, staying on The Bridge with Aunt. I may well have stayed on a while longer at Conigre House because I do remember going off with grandmother on her bowls trips.

The family had two other holidays during this period, which turned out to be the only family holidays we ever had together. One was at Normans Bay near Hastings, where we stayed in a caravan in a clearing between mine fields on the beach. These minefields still hadn't been cleared from the beaches 3 years after the war had ended, so that holiday was a bit bleak to say the least. There was also a foghorn that would be sounding all night from a nearby lighthouse. The other holiday was in 1950, when we had a week at Margate, staying in a boarding house. This was quite good because I learned to swim and play the machines in the funfair, but after this I was to spend all my holidays at Frome.

In the early part of 1950 my Gran at Conigre had been taken ill. I had been there at Easter but had known nothing about it, and a short while afterwards she died. Her funeral was on Cup Final day in the May.

Back in London, I had watched the match on my friend's 9" television, but Dad though, went to the funeral and had to give his ticket away and miss the match.

There was no point now in Grandad remaining at Conigre House, so during the summer he prepared to move out. By the August he had arranged an auction of all the house furniture. I was there when Mr Quick of Cooper and Tanner conducted the sale, and was very saddened to see all the furniture that I knew so well being auctioned off, part of all of us was going forever. I was given a pair of binoculars as a memento.

Grandad and the black cat called Tim were then to move back to The Bridge and stay with his sister. They had never had a strong relationship and now it was going to be tested to the full, he was a very forceful character and she was quite timid.

After this I spent every Easter and summer holiday with them until I left school, not one day of any of these holidays did I spend in London, and in 1950 I was only eight.

Soon the London life was to take me over, and it would only be at holiday times that I would get released to my other life in Somerset. For life in London, you cannot help but appreciate the range of activities going on. The buildings and the transport system, the buses and tube trains become part of you. On top of that there is a great advantage of living in Holborn, because it is right in the centre.

By this time rebuilding was taking place over most of the bombsites, with offices and typical post-war blocks of flats rising up. My friends and I would still have some of these to play on, and on Guy Fawkes Night there would be a huge bonfire on the largest remaining bombsite in Theobalds Road.

1951 was celebrated by the Festival of Britain exhibition on the south bank of the river. This is close to where the Millennium Wheel is now situated. The idea of the festival was to show that Britain was now out of the grips of the austerity years, and with rationing being phased out, things were shown to be distinctively better. The exhibition was very cheerful with bright colours everywhere, and it made quite a difference to those 'black and white' days of the period.

We lived just a mile from the Festival, so I got to know it very well. Most of the exhibits were to show new inventions and how developments could affect our lives. There was not much about rail travel and how that may be influenced by the new diesel locomotives. In fact they had on display one of the new Britannia Class of steam locomotives. No. 70004 'William Shakespeare.'

London was known for its peasouper fogs, where it was impossible to see more than a few feet in front of your face. The cause of these was the mass of sulphuric smoke coming from coal fires, domestic and industrial. The inside of my nose was all black after I had been out in these. Some time later the worst ever 'smog' appeared. This was in the December of 1952 and many thousand deaths were attributed to it. It was so bad that new legislation soon got brought in to limit smoke emissions. But then it was all part of London life, and all the buildings were blackened by the soot.

four

Summer 1951

I had travelled down to Frome on my own during this year, and although I was only nine I was quite independent enough to do that. It set the pattern that was to be the same every time.

Dad saw me off at London and, unlike now, the trains to Weymouth would stop at Frome. But I could speed up the journey by travelling on the Cornish Riviera Express, the premier train of the Great Western. This departed from London at 10.30 each morning and was always pulled by a 'King' Class locomotive, the best steam engines of the region. The first scheduled stop for the train was Plymouth.

As Frome is about a hundred miles short of Plymouth I was to take advantage of one of the great novelties of the old Great Western Railway, something that was continued after nationalisation of the railways in 1948.

This was the innovation of a 'slip carriage,' which was attached to the back of the train. This slip coach had a separate guard in it, and he could disconnect the coach from the rest of the train while it was travelling at full speed, and then bring it to a halt with a brake. This would be done just before Westbury and there would be a tank engine standing by to pull the carriage into Westbury Station. There it would be attached to the back of a slower train bound for Weymouth. The whole journey would take about two and a half-hours; I would absorb every moment of it.

Grandad met me at Frome Station, and the Trowbridge bus was in the forecourt waiting. There is something very reassuring about a double-decker bus standing outside a railway station. The Express Dairy was in full swing with the noisy churns being unloaded from the lorries into the factory, the hum of the processing going on within it.

This was about the only time he ever met me at the station because it was dinnertime, and he would need to be at home cooking it. Auntie was there but she was never allowed near the kitchen. Grandad had become an expert cook in his old age, he had even 'modernised' with a pressure cooker. His life was centred on gardening and cooking.

Auntie was still active at that time in the running of her hat shop, although she was a bit absentminded. Sometimes she would forget to lock up the shop and a policeman would be knocking on the door in the middle of the night.

I would be very ready for the dinner after my journey, and already be affected by the fresh air.

Grandad had taken a new garden, which was a strip of ground beside the Frome to Bristol branch line and as soon as dinner had finished, I was pressing him to go down there.

To get there we would go down Willow Vale as far as the railway bridge, then climb up on to the line and walk towards the station. The garden was the strip between the line and the field wall on the left. For a time he also cultivated the strip of land on the 'church' side of the railway. It was a lovely spot, and so peaceful, until a train went by that is, then the sound filled the whole area.

I would spend my time waiting for a train to come along, and have a penny ready to put on the line for the train to squash. I was going to be in Frome for a month and would relish every minute. This became my second home, and I would go everywhere with Grandad, sometimes going off on my own on little adventures when he was working or cooking the dinner.

The rest of the family came down for a while towards the end of my stay. Walks and coach trips were then on the agenda. Dad would take me to all the railway places. My favourite was to go up to Clink, and then we would walk along the railway embankment to Rodden footbridge. Then the return journey would be back down the hill and across the field to Wallbridge and back through Willow Vale.

In days gone by, Grandad had been on the Town Council at Frome. One of his stories, is that he instigated the building of the road that cuts across from Wallbridge to link up with Rodden Road. He said it was named Swain's Lane, but I think that he was being rather fanciful. I've never seen it ever written down as that, it now seems to be called New Road on one town map.

He was also a Fuel Officer during the war and kept the job right up until 1952. His office was in the brick building just opposite the station approach road, the former Wallbridge Hotel. He had a reputation for being rather mean with his coal allocations during war. This was obviously ingrained into him, because when I was with him for Easter he would only have about two pieces of coal on the fire.

That August we went on a couple of Crown Tours trips. The later one was with all the family and was to Weymouth. Grandad would prepare an elaborate picnic for us to have on the beach. He cut and wrapped the sandwiches so well that it was almost an art form, every item was wrapped like a parcel and tied with string. His pride in his workmanship never left him. He'd serve these to everyone on the beach in the same way that he would carve and serve a joint on the Sunday dinner table.

It was very pleasant at Weymouth, with the curved beach, donkey rides and a Punch and Judy show. The steamers would leave occasionally for Jersey and this was a good sight. Dad would take me round to the docks and see a little steam train, actually going through the town, on rails cut into the surface of the road. This train connected the town station with the docks, it was a remarkable sight going through the streets of Weymouth.

When I had been on holiday before at Conigre House, Nanny went off on some trips with her Bowling Club and I went on one of these with her. This was on a Crown Tours coach, or 'Sharry' as she had called it. After the war they ran an old austerity coach, which had wooden slatted seats. A little while later though, it had disappeared and a nice Bedford had joined their fleet (just like the one featured in the film 'Titfield Thunderbolt'). This time the family were on this coach and it was a favourite of mine. It had its own very distinctive engine sound, which once heard was never forgotten. Of course it was painted in the distinctive yellow livery, just like all the rest of the Crown Tours coaches.

On our coach trips, Grandad had the bright idea of giving us children a type of I-Spy competition. While in the Fuel Office he had typed out a list of things for us to try and see from the coach. It turned out that we had all the same things on our lists. I can remember two items, a combine harvester and a church clock that had stopped.

By the next year there was an I-Spy in the News Chronicle. Someone called Big Chief I-Spy put this out and books were on sale covering different subjects. If you got enough points you could send the book off to Big Chief and win a feather. Also, he would print coded messages in the News Chronicle and there was a codebook to help break these codes. He finished off his article with the coded message XXODHUNTINGGO.

Anyhow I think that Grandad was a bit miffed about all this, because we had all preferred these to his, and he had thought of it first.

Looking back on it Big Chief I-Spy had a good thing going for himself. Because he had hoards of children scouring the country, and providing information of the whereabouts of all the little historic curiosities that make this country so interesting. He must have built up a wealth of information.

At the end of that holiday I went home with the family on the train. We had to change at Westbury and wait while an engine was put onto our train. There was a line of engines all steamed up in the parallel bay platform. Dad and I were wondering which one was going to pull us. It turned out to be a Hall Class 'Saint Martin.'

five

Easter 1952

It was early in 1952 when we received a letter from Auntie. She told us that at the back of her shop there was a Kingfisher coming and going. This at first didn't make much impression on us, until we saw one of these in the new I-Spy book called I-Spy Birds.

A Kingfisher had a page all to itself and was worth 40 points. No other bird in the book was worth more. The book said that it was a very shy bird and that all you might see of it was a flash of blue as it darted away up stream. Jill, my elder sister, and I were going to Frome for Easter and now we couldn't wait to see this bird and enter the find in the I-Spy book.

Below the bridge there are two main arches, and in those days the back area was very secluded. Between the two arches at the back, there was the timber structure on stilts, which was a relic from the former tailoring business. The hat shop was directly over the left-hand arch as seen from the front. The view out the back windows was over the secondary route of the river, not the main stream. It was also very shallow, in fact ideal for a Kingfisher. So, at the back of the shop, there was the best view to watch the whole proceedings.

We duly arrived, and yes there it was. It had a free run of the area, with a choice of perches at low or high level. There was an overflow pipe from the side flank of next door, which was constantly dripping. The Kingfisher would often have a little sip of this before diving down to catch a little fish and then dart off up the river, (in a flash of blue). Sometimes he would return to the same perch holding the fish and we would get a real close up look.

The Kingfisher hung around for a couple of years, until the river became polluted. Factories had begun to dump waste in the river and one-year it was running with a white froth on top. This effectively ended the visits of the Kingfisher because we never saw one again after that.

I never did see inside the old tailoring extension. There was a way through to it from a cellar, but this was cluttered up. The door had to be kept tightly shut, to keep out any vermin. That extension stayed desolate and undisturbed for over forty years after the close of the business.

It was demolished in the mid-eighties to make way for a residential extension. The whole of the back area was opened out in 1970 with a footbridge being installed from the car park to the cattle market. One of the most secretive parts of the town had then been exposed.

Frome Town Band had a building on the south side at the back, which faced out onto the river. This was where they practised a couple of times a week. Later on though, it got burnt down, and that was the end of that. Auntie saw it all happen from her bedroom window.

Grandad and Auntie had a regular home help. She was Mrs. Whitmarsh who was long serving and ever loyal. Her husband worked for British Railways and drove around Frome making deliveries. His vehicle was what was called a 'Mechanical Horse.' That is a goods vehicle of a type that was introduced in the thirties with the aim to replace the horse and cart, and that is how it got its name. They were very common in the fifties, that decade being their heyday. They were generally quite slow, and had no reverse gear and no self-starter, and with their very throaty sound they added great atmosphere to the streets. This one would operate out of the station goods yard, and have a setting down point somewhere behind Woolworth's in the Market Place.

Auntie was a dear, and a much-loved person by everyone, except that is by Grandad. Nobody had a bad word to say about her, she was always giving me a few shillings. Once I said to her 'Auntie, you know, I've never had one of those white five pound notes,' and she gave me one. For every sale that she made in her shop, she would record it in a Boots Scribbling Diary. Somedays nothing got entered in it at all and she would have had a completely blank day. One day she sat by her shop window and counted the vehicles that crossed the bridge. She came up with the answer that there were over a thousand an hour at the busiest time.

Our fourth meal of the day was supper. This was a sit down meal that begun at 8pm sharp. Sometimes this could be quite an ordeal, as Jill discovered on this trip. Mackerel was served and Jill was sure that she could see little things crawling around in it. Now Grandad was not too impressed if anyone left anything from one of his meals. On this occasion she was in trouble. She was in total fear of leaving anything and didn't know what to do. As was quite normal in these situations, Auntie helped her out by eating some of it. Grandad's eyes hardened, as he detested her doing this and his glare could kill. But this time they got away with it, although a year later my younger sister was not to be so lucky.

Auntie was quite a dashing lady in her time. She was once married but nobody knew what happened to her husband. We have since found out that he went to the Boer War and never came back. After this she had taken over the hat shop at No. 5, and run it on her own for about sixty years.

Her married name was Neale but there was once a mis-spelling that called her Peale. The name stuck and forever after that she was Peale to everyone or Aunt Peale to the children. When we were young children we called Grandad, Popeye, this must have been hilarious on a coach with us noisy children calling them Popeye and Aunt Peale.

In the early twenties, Auntie drove around in a little three-wheeler car. She must have had some social life going in Bournemouth, because Dad tells me she was going down there very often at that time and would never take him with her. One time though, she had a blow-out in the rear tyre of the little car at Pepperbox Hill and ended up in Salisbury Hospital.

This visit had given us a new look at night, because outside our bedroom window there was a new streetlight. All the old tall lampposts had been removed, and had been replaced by orange sodium lights, which were quite strange.

six

Summer 1952

By this time I was very much into the routines of my holidays in Frome, it was very much my second home. I had spent my infancy there and gone to school, now it was holidays at every opportunity, and I loved the place.

Mealtimes with Grandad were legendary. Everything had to start exactly on time, with breakfast at 9am, dinner at 1 o'clock, tea at 5 o'clock and supper at 8. Also there was cheese and biscuits at 11am and a cup of Bourn-Vita or Cocoa just before bed. He had known how to eat well, and all the Victorian habits had prevailed.

At dinner, all the vegetables would be brought from the kitchen in bowls, and he would cut the meat off a joint and serve everyone in turn. We all had to wait and start eating together, and to give him credit it was superb, everyone seemed to have the right amount because leftovers were definitely not permitted.

For the second course, it was a pudding or pie, and the fruit pies were second to none. He or Mrs Whitmarsh would prepare these in deep tins, with the freshest fruit. These again he would serve up on the table. I can't remember having custard and never ever cream, but it certainly didn't need it. A bees-knee of cheese would finish it. My mother said that she liked me going to Frome because it fattened me up. But I was always small, and later on when I was 20 my weight was only 9 Stones.

There was always a tin of Andrews Liver Salts, which Grandad sometimes took to aid his digestion. I was always quite fascinated at the way that this would fizz in a glass. I once threw a whole tin into the river to see if the river would go all frothy. It didn't.

I would go off on little walks by myself while everybody was busy, making sure of course to be back on time for dinner. There was always something to investigate down the river or along the branch-line.

Wednesday was market day, and the cattle market was just around the corner from us. Grandad would have an early look in the salerooms at the hard goods or fruit etc. Later he would go back and bid for something. Once when I was with him, there was some bidding for a large punnet of raspberries. The bidding had gone from sixpence and then to a shilling and Grandad came in with a bid of 'FOUR SHILLINGS.' The place went dead and the hammer quickly came down with the auctioneer saying 'Yours sir.' On the way out I was looking questioningly and Grandad said, 'Well it killed the bidding didn't it' and he hurried off to finish the dinner. He had always bought from auctions, so he obviously knew what he was doing, and was in a hurry to finish the dinner.

Another time I saw him coming away from the market with a chicken in his hand and its wings were still flapping. He had bought the chicken and wrung its neck there and then. Which had caused some consternation with those people around and about.

After Tea, Grandad would nearly always go to his garden. We would be walking along Willow Vale and this little fellow called Eustace Mitchell would come up and say 'Got a fag Fred,' and Grandad would always give him one of his roll-ups. He grew his own, and rolled them up in a Rizla machine. I would also do some for him and Eustace knew this and would ask me. I would have one to give him, that was made with 4 filter tips and just a little bit of tobacco, he didn't ask me again after that.

Down at the garden it was so peaceful. Occasionally a train would go by and I would add to my collection of flattened pennies. On Sunday evenings the bells from St.John's Church rang across the fields from their lofty perch, and this was very atmospheric. It was a very peaceful world.

The old Clink railway bridge before it was demolished to make way for a new structure. The signal indicates that the westbound express train is clear to proceed along the 'loop' line.

View of the back of The Bridge in 1974 from the new footbridge. What was previously a secretive area is now open to view. The timber structure on stilts, which was the workshops for tailoring business is still standing at this time, although it had been unused since 1936.

A view of Willow Vale from an old postcard. The little wooden footbridge was swept away in one of the pre-war floods.

Conigre House with the lawned front garden and the Mulberry Tree in the foreground.

Two very interesting old picture postcards show views across The Bridge and into the Market Place. In the picture above, two chimneys are seen in the distance. The thin one is from the boiler of the Victoria Swimming Baths, and the tall one belonged to the Edmundson Power Station. Horsey and Witcomb brush and hardware shop is in the foreground, next to this is the jewellery shop of Mr. Thick. The third shop in the terrace sold fancy goods. The man on the pavement is standing outside Swaine & Son tailoring shop. The large ornamental lamp standard was made by the Cockey Company at the time when electricity replaced gas for street lighting.

The same view but now forward in time to around 1950. The shop with the vertical blinds is Mrs Neale's hat shop, and beyond that was Woodmancy's music shop. The lorry is from The Frome United Brewery making a delivery to the Bridge Hotel. The cooling tower of the Water Works is visible on the horizon.

A view of Catherine Hill beside the high pavement. One of the many picturesque streets in the town and the location of the Swaine tailoring business before the move to The Bridge in 1840. The hill was the main route out of town on the south side, before Bath Street was cut in the 1820's.

The newsagent shop in Cheap Street was always the centre of attraction. Especially for the men who waited for the evening paper to get the football and racing results.

Seven

London 1953

It was the year of the Coronation, Everest had been climbed, and Sir Gordon Richards had won the Derby. It was also the year when I left Primary School to move on, and we also moved into a more spacious flat in Bury Place, Holborn.

I was in the final year at St George's Primary School, preparing for the 11-plus examinations. The results from this would determine my future education. The brightest pupils would go on to Grammar schools and the average or below would go to Secondary Modern Schools.

I attained what they called a central margin, which is a result that is not quite a good pass but also not a failure. With this grade the headmaster can make an assessment on you. The headmaster had a meeting with mother, and advised that there was a new experimental type of school system, which was known as comprehensive. He said that this would suit me better than trying for a Grammar school place. He was right; I would really have struggled if I had got into the low end of a Grammar school, because I was not that bright and much preferred playing games to doing school work.

One of my friends did worse than me in his 11-plus, but his father hounded the headmaster into getting him a Grammar School placement. My friend ended up with masses of homework, and was continually struggling; I was thinking that I was quite pleased with myself for missing all that.

My new school was three miles away in north London, and was the opposite extreme from before. The first day at a new school is an awesome experience, and I was going from a little primary school to a big experimental Haverstock Comprehensive School with 1500 pupils.

I was in a class of 40 children, split equally between boys and girls. It was going to be a new experience to have a different teacher for every subject, when previously the one teacher would take us for everything. The range of subjects, which included French, art, and a full morning of woodwork fascinated me. It was a school where everyone could find a stream that suited their abilities, whether that would be academic, technical, clerical, or into a stream that would leave school at 15.

It suited me well and I filtered into the technical stream at the age of 13. I hesitate to think how I would have got on in a Secondary Modern school where there were no options. Some bright kids ended up in these after being let down by the 11-plus exams, and then fell well short on getting a good education.

My friend would join me in going to watch the Arsenal football team, as this was our real passion. I still sometimes went with dad, but this was usually now to 'away' games.

As well as going to football matches, my friend would join me in going around some of the big railway stations and checking out the steam engines.

At Kings Cross Station they had just re-introduced all the old Nestles chocolate vending machines. These had been removed during wartime and had not been replaced until this time due to rationing. Many a foreign coin passed through these, as they were fully tested out by the boys, including us.

They were quite heady days, I had the freedom to come and go as I pleased, and would sometimes not come home until after the night mail-train had departed from Kings Cross at 10 p.m.

eight

August 1954

The end of first year examinations from my London school had left me well placed in my class. I had finished 10th in the class of forty pupils, and was quite pleased with this. I had my school report in my pocket and was well set to be going off on holiday the next day.

Travelling down to Frome from London, I was again on the Cornish Riviera Express. The guard slipped the back coach off as usual just before Westbury and brought the carriage to a halt. The little tank engine was there as usual to pull us into Westbury station. We then would be hitched to the back of a stopping train, and a little while later we would be off, with the next stop of the train being Frome.

I had to walk from Frome station, the mile or so into the town centre. Walking becomes a feature of small town life, and it can seem such a drudge. But at least I had dinner to look forward to.

On arriving, the only change in the house that was noticeable was that Grandad had changed his old sunburst radio for a new Bakelite set.

My grandfather was giving up the wireless set that had been with him for about twenty years. It was the one that took him through the war years and from which he heard all the mighty speeches made by Churchill in those darkest days ten years before.

That old set had a certain fascination for me as an inquisitive kid. There were names of the available radio stations written on a plate behind a little glass window on the set. There was a button, which could be turned which moved a little wire across a dial to pick out any of the stations. Only three British radio stations could be received at the time, they were the Light Programme, the Home Service and the Third Programme. There was also a station called Hilvershum, but I had no idea what or where that might be.

Radio was always the only entertainment medium in the household. Never was there a television set or a gramophone, only news

41

or studious programmes got heard in this household, with Grandad liking programmes such as 'Twenty Questions.'

I was starting to listen to the popular music of the time and had an interest in what was going on, although there were a very limited number of music programmes on during the day. Not like later on when wall-to-wall pop music could be heard on BBC Radio 1. That was the programme, which came about because of the insatiable appetite for music that the young people had in the sixties.

Although not at number 5 The Bridge, radio programmes could be heard coming out of just about every house as people looked forward to their Sunday lunch in the fifties. This was a time when music was played and the most popular programme was 'Two Way Family Favourites,' which was scheduled at noon on the Light Programme. The opening music was to the tune of 'With a Song in my Heart' and this music certainly reminded you that it was Sunday, just to make sure, it was followed by the Billy Cotton Band Show.

The idea of Family Favourites was to provide a request show to link people at home with loved ones in the armed forces overseas. Later on the programme expanded to provide requests for people who had emigrated.

It was the time of National Service and there were very many mothers putting in requests for their sons who were stationed in Germany or other places where there was a British military presence. Current hit songs generally got played and these included such artists as David Whitfield, Alma Cogan or Vera Lynn.

The requests got mentioned with a little message, which said things to remind the recipient that 'the two years will soon go by,' which must have made them feel even more homesick. The address of the squaddie or airman was always an overseas British Forces postal number, such as: BFPO 32-Cyprus, BFPO 453-Gibraltar, BFPO 271-Cologne. Code words for all those far off locations.

The Billy Cotton Band Show would start with him shouting out his catch phrase 'WAKEY! WAKEY!' and then be a half hour of band music with his regular guests Kathy Kay and Alan Breeze. It was all very regular and every Sunday morning had the same feel to it with these two shows running on for many years.

The early Norman Doorway at Lullington Church.

It was in the late fifties that the youngsters were to get hold of electric guitars and drums and change the face of popular music forever. People like Cliff Richard and Elvis Presley became the new face of music and all those sentimental crooners from before found that their time was up, they then faded off the scene. Again it is an example of the times changing dramatically at that point in time. I did later find out that Hilvershum was a station in Holland. It must have been one that could have been easily received in this country back in the thirties.

This holiday was to be a revelation to me because Grandad bought me a bike. I had never had one before and couldn't ride.

There was this small bike in the saleroom near King Street, which Grandad had seen, and he asked me if I fancied it. Well, it was completely out of the blue and of course I said yes, and we went along to the sale. The lot came up and Grandad duly bid. The hammer came down at one shilling and sixpence (7.5p), and we had it.

I was walking home pushing a bike with flat tyres. We went into Halford's shop in the Market Place, and bought a puncture outfit. With some tyre levers and a can of oil, it wasn't long before Grandad had it up and running.

The next thing was to learn to ride. We went up North Parade and into Windsor Crescent, then he spent the next half-hour trying to get me going. Grandad held the saddle and ran along holding me until I had finally got the hang of it and could keep going. Grandad was talking to some friends of his so I went off on a ride up to Clink Railway Bridge, about a mile away.

My favourite spot was now within my reach, I was in clover. Back I went, and from then on I was going everywhere, my days of dependency were over. This little bike was to serve me well for over 2 years, I went all over the place on it, and when I was in London I travelled the 3 miles to school on it.

Morning was my best time to cycle up to Clink, Grandad had now finally retired from the Fuel Office, he would be at the garden and then sorting out dinner. I would be up there watching all those great trains rushing by. In early August there would be a succession of 14 carriage trains taking holidaymakers west. The Torbay Express would go through on its way to Paignton before then going down the single track to Kingswear. At about 12-20 the Cornish Riviera would go through, lighter after shedding its slip coach at Westbury. All these would be pulled by a 'King' or a 'Castle' the elite steam loco's of the old Great Western, which later became the Western Region of British Railways. The all-purpose 'Halls' or sometimes the impressive 'Counties' with their straight nameplates would take a lesser train or be substituting on an express train if necessary. The 'Halls' usually took the stopping trains into Frome Station from the loop line.

It was a very tranquil atmosphere up there. For most of the time it would be almost silent, except for the sound of birds or grasshoppers. The breeze would make a slight whining sound through the telegraph wires. Then there would be a couple of rings in the signal box opposite, the signalman would pull a couple of levers, a signal would fall and the expectancy level rise. A minute or two later one of those monsters would come thundering through shattering the peace, before it would fade into the distance and all would be quiet again.

I didn't know it at the time, but the fifties was the last great decade of steam on the railways. It all carried on into the sixties but it was fast running down with the diesels taking over. The decline of the steam engine was something that I didn't want to witness. In the sixties, steam engines were being scrapped in their thousands, and it was a very sad time. Some of these great engines have survived and been restored by enthusiasts. They now run on preserved lines around the country, including the Paignton to Kingswear branch, which is one of the best.

I would check engine numbers in my Ian Allan spotter's book, and be very pleased to have gained some new engines that may have strayed off their usual runs. Sometimes I would be waiting for a train and the time would be getting very close to 1 o'clock. The dash back to the bridge for dinner would occasionally be quite frantic.

My bicycle gave me another dimension to my interests. I was able to get around and see all different places. I had the Ordnance Survey one-inch to the mile map No. 166, and could travel around picking out places of interest and go and see them. A little map measure showed me the distances, so off I would go. I still had some

45

I-Spy books, two of which had special interest, they were, I-Spy 'History,' and I-Spy 'The Unusual.' Over the next summer or two I was to get to know where all the places of interest were in the area. Whether that be the stocks at Faulkland, the mounting steps at the old George pub in Norton St Philip, the lock up, tithe barn and pack-horse bridge at Bradford upon Avon, or the Norman doorway to the little church at Lullington. All got marked down in the books and the points mounted up. Being on my own, all sorts of intrigues went on inside my head as I rode along. I knew all the roads and country lanes so well, that just to look at the names of the places on the map gave me a tingle of delight.

The area around Frome provides a wealth of places to discover for a boy cyclist.

The old George Inn at Norton St Philip. Note the mounting steps at the front.

nine

Frome owes a huge dept of gratitude to one of its former Manu-facturers. I am talking about the firm of E.C. Cockey & Sons Ltd, who first made church bells from the 16th Century, and then later branched into all kinds of ironwork. Finally they ended up at the Garston Works towards the end of the 19th. Century.

They were the makers of all the Frome lamp standards, and had made about a dozen big lamp standards at the time when electric-ity came to the town. These standards spread out from The Bridge, along the Market Place, up Bath Street and along Christchurch Street to Badcox.

All of these were phased out in the early fifties to make way for sodium lighting. I have no great distress about this because they wouldn't have given the suitable spread of light, which is necessary for modern day traffic. But it would have been nice if one or two had been kept.

The piece-de-resistance though from the Cockey Company are the smaller lamp standards. Even from the age of infancy I could appreciate these. When we were coming and going from Conigre House, there was the one at the top of Cork Street just across from the Singer Factory. This is the sort of thing that you can only really appreciate when it has gone, and that particular one has gone.

Thankfully though, most of the others in town have survived albeit with different lamps. It might be eco-friendly to have fluores-cent lighting, but when I was a young boy these had a single tung-sten bulb with a little double reflector over the top. I thought that they were the most beautiful of things.

Just who inspired or designed them we do not know. They may have been an accumulation of earlier designs, which came together. But Frome has got them and should be grateful. They are unique in design and unashamedly decorative, they are the ultimate in pretty wrought ironwork.

These small lamp standards (they are above being called lamp-posts) originally were made for gas, and early photographs show this.

It was probably a dozen or more years into the twentieth Century before they were converted to electricity. We only have to go out and look to see how they appear now. But it was how they were with the single bulb and double reflector that I remember. They gave a lovely twinkly light, and it was well spread. The changeover when it happened was well intended with low energy fittings, but the new lamps do not suit the standards so well, and it is doubtful if they give better light. We do though still have the main parts, and I have no doubt that over the centuries to come there will be more variations of the lamps.

Singers factory in Frome never had any association with Singer Sewing Machines, that was a completely different company.

The factory adjoining the car park in Frome actually made statues. This included some very famous examples, one of which is the Boudicca statue on the Embankment, beside Westminster Bridge in London. A fine statue it is, but there are no reins to the horses. Perhaps that is something that cannot be made in a foundry. Another statue they made was the one of King Arthur in Winchester.

The making of bronze statues is a very interesting operation, and if the factory was still in production, it would have been fascinating to have a tour around and learn all about those procedures.

During wartime the factory was turned over to the war effort, and castings for war equipment would have been made.

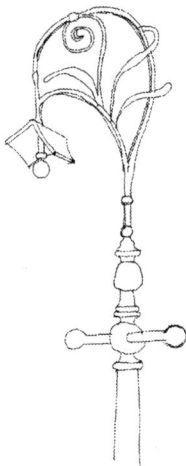

ten

August 1954

I was now a cyclist and the bike went everywhere with me, and this included on the train going from London to Frome. However, there was a considerable hike in the fare for the bike when the journey went over a hundred miles. It so happened that the journey from Paddington to Westbury was under the hundred, and to go on to Frome put the journey over the hundred. So I set a trend which went on until I left school, I got off at Westbury and cycled the seven miles to Frome. This was a very enjoyable experience and gave me a bit of exercise after the long journey on the train.

I got to know the route very well, sometimes going via Dilton Marsh, and sometimes through Chapmanslade. Always coming into Frome along the Clink Road.

Passing through Westbury Leigh I often heard the train from Westbury to Salisbury climbing the steep Dilton Bank. This had a steam engine at the front and a banking engine at the rear, both working very hard to get up that incline.

The timing of my arrival at Frome brought me in just before one o'clock, (I would also have had a stop off at Clink railway bridge if I was ahead of time), and after the journey I was very looking forward to one of Grandad's dinners, not to mention the six weeks stay that I was about to have.

Dad and Angela (my younger sister) also came down to Frome towards the end of my stay. This meant that we would go off on some more Crown Tours trips, and Auntie would be involved, which pleased her, as she would not come with Grandad and me when we went out.

Dad was a very keen Bridge player and at every opportunity he would be arranging a game. Mum also played and so did Auntie and Grandad. On this one occasion they had also invited a cousin Catherine Trotman, and also Mrs Millett, an old friend from the Beckington farming family.

Catherine was the daughter of Lucy Rawlings of the eminent Frome family who were card makers to the woollen trade. Lucy had married Edward Vaughan Trotman who was part of the brewing family of the town. One of the Millett family had also married a Rawlings (Samuel Tovey) at the end of the eighteenth century. Grandad and Auntie's mother was also born a Rawlings (Jane), so all the families are well connected.

Both the Trotmans and the Rawlings have well documented family histories and both families trace their origins well back into the nobility of the twelfth century. Apparently it was only the Noble families who kept any records before the fifteenth century. Catherine showed these to me later and it helped me greatly in compiling our extended family tree.

At this game of Bridge Mrs Millett asked if I would like to go out and visit her farm in Beckington. This invitation was gratefully accepted, and my visits to Priors Court Farm were to go on for many years.

By this time I was becoming a strong cyclist and I would think nothing of going off for long rides. I could also get up all the hills of Frome on the bike, and it was good to explore places that had only been accessible by bus when I had been accompanied, such as Cley Hill or Westbury White Horse.

The area around Frome is excellent for walking, and when Dad and the others were there we would all go off somewhere. We would take a bus out and take a walk back by a different route. The sort of walks we took were along the following lines;

- A bus to Old Ford, and a look around Bonnyleigh Wood and then back through the grounds of Orchardleigh House.

- Take the Shepton Mallet bus to Vallis, and then walk along beside the river and through the quarry and meet up with the Bristol-Frome branch line and follow that back via Spring Gardens. (Grandad would always make a point of washing his hands in the river mud at Vallis, and remark on how clean the river mud would get your hands).

- A bus up to Fricker Lane, before Corsley Heath. Then look for mushrooms in the nearby fields and then walk back through Wallbridge and Willow Vale.

- Take a bus to Nunney, with a look around the castle. At that time there was a nice new bus shelter, which had just been built with a thatched roof. The walk back could well have taken in the Frome Park and a round of putting.

I duly took up Mrs Millett's invitation to visit her farm at Beckington, and on that first occasion I was to stay the night, although in my many visits over the following years this was the only time that I stayed.

I cycled out to Beckington, and up Goose Lane the half mile to Priors Court Farm, and was quite in awe of the place. She had over a hundred acres, with a herd of about sixty cows for milking. She was quite elderly and had two unmarried middle-aged sons, Jeffrey and John who ran the farm. There was also the help of a chief assistant Mr Bennett, and some farm hands who lived in the tied cottages down Goose Lane. I was to become good friends with John and would go around with him.

The farm smells were very intoxicating. I quickly became addicted and was certain that there was never going to be anything else I wanted to do in my life except farming.

Mrs Millett had seven cats, some of which were semi-wild and would stay well clear when a stranger like me was around. The tame cats names were Oily, who was so named because he fell in a drum of oil, then there was Wee who was so named because he was so small, and Lulu who slept on my bed with me that night. When I woke up in the morning I had midge bites over my body which was pretty uncomfortable.

Mrs Millett talked to all of the cats and asked them what they had been doing. This was without getting much reply so she suggested to them what they had been up to, and scolded them if one had caught a bird. It was also quite common for one of the hens to stroll in and peck at the cats bowl.

Being a boy from the City everything was so new to me, I did not even know that cream came from the top of the milk, and they kept saying that 'He's from the city you know.'

Things like going and collecting eggs from the various nooks and crannies where the free running hens laid them, was quite exciting. Mrs Millett also made her own butter, and this also was an eye opener. It was all so fresh, it was unbelievable.

John gave me a ride around on one of the tractors the next day, and in the following years I was to drive the little Ferguson myself.

These Ferguson tractors were first introduced in the 1930's and revolutionised farming. It was the first piece of machinery with which the driver could raise or lower an implement attached to the back from his driving seat. So useful was this that many farmers decided at that time to finally phase out the horse and become mechanised. The one on Priors Court Farm was a post war version built in the 1950's.

The other tractor on the farm was an old Fordson. This was a complete brute in comparison to the Fergie, but it was also a glorious piece of machinery. It had one of those round metal seats with holes in it.

I had lights on my bike, and on the journey home I was to experience riding in the pitch dark for the first time. It amazed me just how much light the battery lamp gave. It was very eerie going down the country lanes surrounded by the almost complete silence.

eleven

August 1955

Grandad was well established with his garden on a strip of land beside the Frome to Bristol branch line, just across the river from Willow Vale.

This was only a few minutes from home and served him well. After walking along Willow Vale he had to climb up onto the railway line and cross the river to get to his strip. Garston Farm was on the other side of the wall and he was now friendly with the farmer and his wife, Mr and Mrs Rossiter. They just kept about a dozen cows, a few hens and some roaming pigs.

While I was there I was able to walk round with Mr Rossiter when he brought in the cows, and be around for the milking. He also rented some fields around Frome, and sometimes he took me there in a huge old Vauxhall convertible that he had.

Mr Rossiter did all the milking by hand sitting on a little three-legged stool. But he was soon to get some modern milking machinery, which he found a bit overwhelming. I sometimes had to help him with a problem or two such as wiring a plug. He would complain about the new fangled things, and was much happier doing things the old way. He even had an old scythe and he was never happier than when out cutting grass with this.

Mrs Rossiter was quite attached to the cows and had given them all names; those that I remember were Emma, Molly, and Belinda. After the milking I would sometimes help him with the mucking out. Mr Rossiter was really pleased with my help and was strongly suggesting that when I leave school I should move down to Frome. This had also crossed my mind, but that was still a few years off.

Grandad and I would have a leisurely stroll down to the garden almost every evening after tea. He would avoid walking down the line if a train was due. One train would leave Frome about 6 o'clock after it had connected with the Channel Island Boat Express from

Weymouth. This train would be steaming quickly as it was on a faster schedule than most.

A few days later we were on a train to Bristol and it was a distinctly slow ride. The sleepy branch line only had another three years to run before it met the same fate as so many and got closed down, on this particular day the service was that of a condemned railway. Our trip was to buy some material from the wholesalers, because Grandad was going to make me a pair of long trousers. I was thirteen then, and so far had only worn shorts.

We got to Bristol and made our way to the wholesalers, which was in a large building, which was also a store. In the trade department they still remembered Grandad; the staff kept calling him 'Mr Swaine of Frome', and made a fuss of him.

We got the grey flannel, buttons and other things. Grandad paid by cheque and after a bit of time in the city and lunch we headed home. Grandad still had a big sewing machine from the tailoring days up in the back room, and certainly still had all his skills, and he made me my trousers.

My younger sister, Angela came down for part of August, and we would go off around places together. Aunt Peale was especially fond of her and so she would take us on a little trip on her half-day or a Sunday, this would have been to Longleat and Shearwater. Auntie had again forgotten to lock the shop and it was fortunate that I had put a 'closed' sign in the window before we left.

Angela liked to read Enid Blyton books and Auntie would buy her one or two of these. I would also read them, and found them quite good. On one occasion, we took one back to WH Smith's bookshop in Bath Street and told the lady that we had been given this one in error. We exchanged it for another that we hadn't read.

Mealtimes were occasionally a bit strained when Angela was there. On a special day we would have a chicken and Auntie would sometimes try and slip Angela an extra piece off of her plate. Grandad was so annoyed with this that he picked up the carcass of the chicken and put the whole thing on Aunt Peale's plate shouting 'Don't be such a silly old fool.' Angela and I were not used to eating much in the evening, but back in the tailoring days this had been their main meal of the day. The habit still stuck and at 8 o'clock every evening we had this set meal. One time he had cooked a stuffed marrow, and it caught Angela out. I must have got through most of mine, but she got really stuck and passed some to auntie. This time he really flipped and called my sister a 'wasteful Girl!'

He soon got over his moments and we didn't take too much notice, but usually it was his sister who got it in the neck. If Auntie ever made a cup of tea, he would take one sip and say. 'The water didn't boil.' He wouldn't accept her doing anything.

The rest of the family then came down for a couple of days, and we had a day out on Crown Tours to Weston. On the way back I must have been showing off. We were driven by a driver called Robbie and I borrowed his peak cap to go around the coach and collect the tips. I put the coins into his pocket, but when he put his cap back on there were still a one of coins still in it. I was then on my knees groping around trying to find it. It was a threepenny bit.

My routine changed when the family went home. Angela went with them, and I was again off to Beckington two or three times a week to see the Milletts.

The football season was about to start, and for Frome Town Football Club this would mean a pre-season friendly or two. I would always try and catch one or two matches before I had to depart back to London.

Frome football was still on a high from getting to the First Round proper of the FA Cup a year ago when they entertained Leyton Orient at Badgers Hill. Dad came down to see that match, but the 'Robins' lost 3-0, and their cup run came to an end. Leyton Orient had an up-and-coming player, Vic Groves in their side who moved to Arsenal a year later.

Frome had a very colourful side at that time. There was the ginger haired goalkeeper Dews, and two lively wingers in Crawford and McManus, and not forgetting the effervescent Tommy Edwards at inside left. Andy Crawford probably created the most publicity, and ambition took him onwards. He moved to Weymouth Town at the end of the season.

When I watched a pre-season friendly match it had seemed ages since the end of the previous football season, almost long enough to forget some of the rules. Things like a foul throw-in, or an indirect free kick being awarded soon brought it all back. Not many people attended and when the ball ran out of play, I would kick it back. I hurt my foot once, not realising how heavy those old leather balls were.

Frome had obviously had a new set of shirts for their cup match the previous year, and they kept these same red and white shirts for the next three years. With each season that passed the shirts slowly faded and by the end of that time they were nearly white. There was no such thing as sponsors then, with the luxury of a new strip every season.

twelve

August 1956

Now I was at the age of fourteen and a very independent person. I had grown out of my small bike, and a second hand tourer had replaced it. Not the apple green Raleigh 'Lenton Sports' model with drop handlebars, which stood outside the little Halford's shop in the Frome Market Place. I did pass longing eyes over that one for more than one summer, but it was not to be, I didn't have the eighteen pounds.

My new bike though, was useful, and served me well for a number of years. The Sturmey Archer 3-speed gear helped with all the hills around Frome, and I could get up every one of them. I was only a small boy. More than once my mother had taken me to the doctor because she thought I was too slight. But I would be off everywhere cycling, and on one occasion I went from Frome to Bath and back, and cycled up every hill - going via Midford and coming back through Limpley Stoke. Grandad was furious when I told him, and said that I would weaken my heart.

My journey down from London on the last Saturday of July now followed the well-proven travel plan. I would get off the train at Westbury Station taking the bike out of the Guards compartment, and then have a quick cup of coffee at the station buffet. This tasted just great in the country air, then I was off on the cycle ride for the final seven miles. So much would I be looking forward to my arrival that I would hardly notice the journey. Quite an opposite effect would be on me for the trip home six weeks later. On my back was a rucksack from scouting activities, and there would be a small case on the carrier.

So precise was I now with my journey that I had told Grandad the exact minute that I would arrive. As I came down North Parade I could see him on the pavement looking at his watch.

The approach to Frome from the top of North Parade was very uplifting. It was the moment that I had arrived and the town was all there before me. The skyline, the buildings and my grandfather all saying. 'Welcome to Frome.'

After my arrival on the Saturday the regular routines soon set in, I would be around to the garden with Grandad and into Mr Rossiter's farm to see the animals. The steam trains kept to their schedules on the branch line, and it was not long before suppertime was upon us, soon to be followed by a nightcap, and off to bed to sleep like a log, in the front bedroom.

When I woke up the following morning, the crisp sounds outside would be immediately noticeable, the individual sounds of the car or bus engines, a bird singing or a dog barking. Such a difference to the centre of London, I was totally intoxicated with it all. The Blue House Clock would strike, as would the church clock, and there was nowhere else on earth where I would rather be.

That Sunday morning I would be off on the bike to the railway junction up at Clink. The usual succession of holiday expresses would be steaming westwards, each crammed full with travellers. This was the first weekend of the factories annual fortnight holiday, so there was a constant procession of these trains. All different types of locomotives would have been commandeered into service, many away from their usual beaten track, helping with the enormous travel operation. I eagerly took down all the numbers, which later I could enter into my spotter's book.

I had to keep a sharp eye on the time, and make sure that by ten to one I was back on that bike, Sunday dinner would be waiting, and I was ready for it. My mother would be thinking of me eating so well, and hopefully being fattened up.

Frome Cricket Club played every Saturday and Sunday afternoons during the summer season, and this Sunday we were off to see them playing at the home ground up at the Cheese Show field. Frome's fixture list would take in the local teams from nearby towns such as Radstock and Trowbridge, and villages like Clandown, Peasedown and Clutton. The matches all were friendlies and did not have a fixed number of overs. The team that went in first batted until tea, and sometimes a little afterwards if they were short of runs. The other team would then try and beat the run total with a finish time of 7-30. If they failed and were not all-out, the match finished as a draw.

Frome had a team full of characters, with Pearce as Captain. Then there was, as I remember, Osborne, Hobbs, Philip Fussell and John Atyeo, the fast bowlers, and the young Tommy Edwards who was master of the 'impossible' run, and regularly ran the opposition into disarray. Of course, Atyeo was the Bristol City footballer, who the previous season had played for England at Wembley, and scored a goal. He did in total play six times for England and scored five goals.

Fussell was a bowler in the Freddie Trueman mould who not only might bowl a side out, but also then contribute with some lusty batting. Many a time would the ball sail over the trees at the end of the ground.

Not often did we go to an 'away' cricket match, but we did go once that summer to Trowbridge to watch the cricket at the their ground, which is lined on one side with Poplar trees.

thirteen

1957 Easter and summer

John Millett, my friend from Priors Court Farm at Beckington had married during the past year. Firstly they had lived at the Old Manse in the middle of the village, and then had moved on to Tellisford where they rented Crab Cottage, which is just up the hill from the river. The village is on the River Frome, and at this stretch, forms the border between Somerset and Wiltshire. The river then runs on to join the Avon near Bradford-on-Avon.

Unknown to me at the time, was that this area had in the past been caught up in the woollen industry. The River Frome had turned many wheels in these parts before the slump of the 1820's had put paid to them. The origins of the cloth mills in Tellisford go back to the 1570's. The little bridge over the river is a packhorse bridge, just as there are other examples in the area. Reminders of the mode of transportation that existed before the Turnpike roads were introduced in the late 1750's.

John now drove a little Morris Minor car, and after he had finished his day's work and all the milking had been done, he would drive off home to Tellisford. I followed on my bike and stayed for an evening. It was quite late when I rode off back to Frome. Down the tiny lanes, with only the bike dynamo lighting to guide me. Sometimes there was moonlight and all the fields were covered in the low silvery light. The only noise was that of my tyres on the road. A far cry from back in Holborn and the city, with its constant light and noise.

On other days on the farm I drove the tractor, I would be harrowing or rolling, never ploughing as this was highly skilled job even with a tractor. On one occasion I was harrowing (breaking down the soil after ploughing) the corner field where the Trowbridge road turns off from the Frome to Bath road. This was a busy road area and there was also activity around the AA box by the corner. I was driving this tractor along and the Trowbridge double-decker bus pulled up at the corner. Everyone on the top deck was watching me, little did they know that I was a London boy on holiday. I had definitely decided that as soon as I was sixteen I would leave school and come down to Somerset and work on the farm.

They had just obtained a new machine on the farm, and nobody knew at the time how much controversy would later surround the product. This was a chemical fertiliser spreader, which was attached to the tractor and would spread little white pellets over the fields. It was to be much later that the hazards of nitrates being spread into the food chain would become apparent, but at that time it was just another aid for the farmers, and I was using it.

John took his family away on trips to the coast in his new car, and I was surprised when he told me that they only averaged a speed of around 28mph for the journey. But this was right, because in those days very few towns had by-passes, all the traffic having to crawl through the centre of each town. They then raced on for a few miles only to be confronted by a long queue and another slow crawl through the next town or village. Even the Crown Tours trips to the coast seem to take an age to get to the destination, but coaches rarely travelled at over 40mph, and this seemed fast. It was not until the coming of the motorways that a new breed of coach came in which could do 70mph, and I thought that was incredible.

Mrs Millett often referred back to her younger days when she could go around in a pony and trap. 'At least you could see things while you gently trotted along,' she said. 'Not like now I'm when sitting in a car, everything is just a blur.'

Back in Frome, things were changing. Auntie had finally decided that it was too much for her to run the shop and had called it a day. She had actually been working right into her mid-eighties. The shop was now let to a Mr Brown, who for a rent of £2 a week was operating as a newsagent. The shop was in a good position, especially on market days with all the passing trade. But later on, with the demise of the cattle market, things were to change again. The letting of the shop did mean that I no longer had access to the back part of the shop overlooking the river, which was a pity. This had been Auntie's little area where she could sit and watch the river at the back. She also liked to sit near the front shop window and look out. It was all to change for her when she closed her shop and it was quite sad.

The Frome cricket team was still performing heroically, and it was a treat to watch. In cricket, every aspect of a person's character gets exposed when they are playing, whether that is a quick temper, a tantrum or an act of bravery or heroism. This is part of the charm of the game, whether it be a top match in a big stadium or one on a village green.

Philip Fussell had a moment that he will be able to tell his grand-children all about. Frome were batting second against one of the villages, and were chasing a big target with the time remaining running out. Frome were down to their bowlers and needed about a hundred runs to win, when Philip stepped in and made 86 runs in 25 minutes. It was an amazing display of a batsman on the attack, making a succession of huge strikes. It was no wonder that he had already made a mark with the county team. I think though, that his farming commitments restricted his county appearances. There were only a small handful of spectators around the ground on that day, and that included Grandad and me. I looked forward to reading the report in the Somerset Standard the following week and rightfully they gave him the credit he deserved.

fourteen

August '58 to August '59

This was the year that I left school, and a good education it had been at my Comprehensive school, although I only excelled at the technical subjects. My GCE passes reflected this as none was in an academic subject. In the technical stream, woodwork was my best subject and I was top of the class. In our family, handicraft ability had jumped a generation. My father's abilities are totally as an academic. I would have been a natural to go into the tailoring business had I been born a generation before, but it was not to be.

As the end of the school year approached, career officers would interview pupils about what they wanted to do. Thoughts were still in my head about going to Frome and to work on the farm, but it was not going to work out. My family had said that the thought of me going to live with my elderly grandfather was not a good idea, and had put me off. I also had a feedback from Grandad that I shouldn't do this, and so I had given up on the idea.

Having had this one thought for a long time, I had no thoughts of an alternative career in my head. I went for a couple of interviews for jobs as a trade apprentice, but the low money did not appeal to me, it was only about £2 a week. I was earning more than that while I was at school doing part time jobs. I finally left school in 1958 without any career in mind, and went down to Frome for a few weeks, I was aware that this was my last chance of an extended holiday there.

I was still on my bike and everything went as it had all those times before, but there were signs of change. The Frome to Bristol branch line had closed, and that had left me a bit depressed. It was not the same at Grandad's garden without the trains.

After about three weeks I thought that I had better go home and get into a job, although I still no idea what that might be.

When it came to my leaving, I was all packed up and ready to say goodbye, and Grandad was in tears. I had never properly realised what my visits had meant to him. We were both very sad, and I did promise him that I would be back again at Easter.

In those days, we did not talk about love or affection. Everything was unsaid, but we knew it was there. Grandad had given me a solid part of my childhood, and had left me with much that I could carry on through my life. I am grateful for that, and although at that time my childhood was over, there were still to be a few more visits for me to The Bridge.

The only idea of where I might look for work was at Odham's Press, who published the Daily Herald newspaper. A distant uncle on my mum's side worked there had said that he might be able to get me in. I did go along and have a look around, but he said to me that there wouldn't be an opening until Christmas, if could I wait until then. The job prospect looked quite interesting and so I thought that I would wait. I had to do something in the meantime so I went along to Euston Station and joined British Railways.

There was a distinct shortage of staff in this labour intensive industry. Steam engines were in the early stages of being phased out, and the first signs of modernisation were in place.

They asked me what I wanted to do, and I just said signalman. Well it was better than cleaning dirty locomotives. I was placed in a signal box at Camden Road as a signalman's assistant, which was at a busy junction on the North London Line. A great variety of trains passed there, with electric passenger services out of Broad Street, and a huge amount of freight. Much of which was steam hauled. A couple of steam hauled passenger trains went out and back to Tring each day.

I was placed with a chatty senior signalman called Ted. Only a senior man could work that junction and manipulate all those goods trains which had to take their turn between the electrics. A new class 20 diesel engine had recently come into service, and these were used on many of the goods trains. Ted was very happy with these as they had quick acceleration and could easily be fed through the junction. Unlike some of the old steam engines, which sometimes had to wait for an hour in a bay platform before being let through.

We had three different shifts, 2pm to 10pm, then 6am to 2pm, and nights, which were 10pm to 6am. These worked in weekly rotation, with for me, the night shift being the best. I could then finish and go to bed until 2 o'clock and then have the afternoon and most of the evening free. Also the money was a bit better - about £4.10.0 (£4.50) a week.

Christmas came along, and there was no sign of employment at the Daily Herald, so I began to think about getting a 'proper job.' This meant going to the Youth Employment Office, and in January 1959 I went along there. I told them that I wanted a job in a drawing office. Again it was the only suitable thing that I could think of.

The answer was that there was no chance of this and would I consider an apprenticeship to become an electrician. On my reply of no, and with me getting ready to leave, the man said 'hold on a minute' and he disappeared. He came back with a pile of cards all seemingly with jobs in drawing offices. It so happened that the top card was for a vacancy in an Architects office, which sounded good enough to me.

I went along for an interview at this little office in Grays Inn, and came away with a position as an office junior at £4 a week. It turned out to be a good move and I was to make my career as an Architectural Technician. I did though pine for the signal box for at least 6 months, but realising that the age of steam was coming to an end, I didn't really want to be there for the last rites.

I kept my promise to Grandad and went down to Frome at Easter, but not by train. I had purchased a 49cc moped and travelled down on that. The journey took four hours and it was cold. The sight of Grandad's coal fire at the end of the journey was most gratifying.

Once there, and dinner was over, I could settle down. This was to be my first time in Frome when I was motorised, whereby I had previously had to rely on pedal power. The moped could get up all the hills, although slowly in the bottom of its two gears. In a day or two I was off to Beckington to show John Millett my little contraption. He was obviously quite impressed because later on he was to get one also. He then could travel between his cottage at Tellisford and the farm on it, while his wife had use of the car.

My stay was only for a few days as I didn't want to use up too much of my 2 weeks annual leave. I did intend to have a holiday with a friend in the summer.

Grandad was showing quite a professional interest in the suit that I had with me, obviously taking him back to his tailoring days. He was quite taken by the cloth covered buttons, also that the trousers had no turn-ups. They were also quite narrow in the leg. Not in the Teddy-boy style of drainpipes, but they tapered to 14", which was narrower than normal men's suits of the time. It also had feature stitching around the collar and lapels, and had a zip fly, which was another new feature. I felt very much the young man about town.

Things were not quite the same at The Bridge. Auntie had become too frail to remain at the house, and had gone into an Old Person's home, she would not survive the next winter there. Without her, Grandad had become less formal with meals and the atmosphere was different. He himself was quite active, although he had started to change things.

He had given up his garden beside the railway, and taken a little plot behind a row of houses in Willow Vale. We were resigned now to my visits becoming shorter. I was making my way in London and developing new interests and making new friends.

In the summer I had traded my moped in for a BSA Bantam 175cc motorbike. My best friend Pete had a similar machine and we spent a few days in Lancashire to visit his relatives near Rochdale. Then I took him to Frome where he stayed for a couple of nights. I stayed a little longer but it was only for about a week.

John Millett was now a family man, and they had left Tellisford and moved to Frome, in a house towards the Berkley area. John's wife was a schoolteacher in Frome and life was moving on for them. There was a distinct hint from Mrs Millett at Beckington that she wanted to give up the farm.

Mr Rossiter at Garston Farm also was slowing down, and he too would be moving out shortly. The end of my era was in sight.

fifteen

End of the farm 1960/1

I had been visiting Priors Court Farm in Beckington for about five years during my summer holidays in Frome, and Mrs Millett was always pleased to see me. But now, with her boys now seemingly unable to carry it on, I heard that she had sold the farm.

Her youngest son John always took me around with him on his rounds, and I did jobs and tractor driving and helping clear up after milking. He now lived at Frome, and for a while had seemed less keen on farmwork. Her elder son Jeffrey, I think was getting fed up with the amount of work that fell on him, so it was probably not surprising that he too wanted to get out.

They accepted a figure of £28.000 for the farm and Mrs. Millett then moved to a cottage in the village. In the late fifties I suppose that they must have thought that this was a good figure. I heard someone say so at the time, but I had my doubts though. I thought that the buyers had got a bargain, after all the farm consisted of over 100 acres of farm, buildings and cottages, much of it abutting Beckington.

Farm people of those times had a big fear of encroachment. This is by the Local Authority or perhaps speculators wanting land for building purposes. If it was the Local Authority, the compensation given to the farmers in a compulsory purchase situation was derisory.

Their farm abutted the edge of Beckington, with the village being about half a mile from the farm buildings. I heard them say on more than one occasion that within 20 years they thought that housing would have crept almost up to them. (The thought of a big road coming through had not crossed anyone's mind, but it is there now).

They were lucky in one respect and unlucky in another. The next decade was to see everything change. They had the benefits of having had such a good quality of life in the days gone by, when farming could be enjoyed, but they were not to get the financial benefits that the changes would bring.

It was also the beginning of the time when artificial fertilisers were coming in more and more. I was there when chemical spreaders appeared, and there was no thought that this may harm the food chain. Certainly after this started and over the next few years, there was a distinct drop in the taste quality of farm products and food generally. The nitrates going into the soil and water were taking a toll.

Other circumstances were causing farmers to stop enjoying their livelihood. The motorway network was spreading, new roads and by-passes cut through farmland everywhere. Inflation was creeping in and farmhands expected parity of pay with other industries. It all helped to change the farmer's attitudes to their profession.

Legislation was shortly to come in that any compulsory purchase by the Local Authority must be paid for at the market price. The next generation of farmers were quickly coming around to the idea that it is much easier to sell for development than it is to work for 16 hours a day in a troubled industry.

This especially gets home when it is realised that 24 houses can be built on an acre of land, and that once a Planning Application is approved the value of that land increases out of all proportion, by about fifty-fold in fact. Land adjoining a town or village was to become one of the most sought after of all commodities. Many of the next generation of farmers became property developers.

sixteen

1962

It was in the September of 1962 when my grandfather died. He was just coming up to his 87th birthday and had lived a long and fulfilled life. I was 20 at the time and had been very close to him for all my life, so obviously I was very sad. I had again visited him twice that year travelling down on a Lambretta motor scooter. It was to be a few months afterwards that I was to get a car, so I had never able to drive him around, which is something that I would liked to have done.

The funeral was effectively to end my association with Frome for the next three decades, except for nostalgic visits. Dad still had his friend John Vincent to visit, who was to continue to run the jewellers shop in Cheap Street until his retirement in the late 1980's.

Once again I was to witness the breaking up of a home. The house had to be sold and the furniture disposed of to various family members. If the house were mine the front room would remain just as I had always known it. My father's sister, Mary from Hereford had a few furniture items, and some came to London with us. I was given the Bakelite Bush radio set.

To me 1962 signifies the end of the old era and the beginning of the new. Frome was beginning to change quite dramatically. Old tracts of the town were being pulled down and much of the Trinity area up behind Conigre House was being developed, and a new shopping development was in hand behind the Market Place in the town centre.

A Motel had appeared on the Bath Road, and horror of horrors, it was selling Watney's beer from London. One of the big attractions of Frome to me was always the complete difference that I would find between the two places and the contrast in life. Now as I rode into town the first thing that I was to see was a Red Barrel sign, just like the one at our local pub in Holborn. Other changes were also happening, new road and housing schemes were in the pipeline, and yellow lines and parking restrictions had appeared.

The government of the day had just issued directives approving slum clearance, and the Frome Town Council, just like every other town and city council in the country, could see no further than to flatten every old building that could be judged as obsolete. Thankfully in the end enough survived to leave us with a good sample of the past.

Motorways have shrunk the country in terms of travel time, and people can commute over long distances. This, and the growth of communication has standardised most things in life. People all across the land now buy the same products from the same chains of shops, and watch the same programmes on television.

We can now be pleased though, with how the town has survived, and is still a very pleasant place. Life has moved on, and since the sixties the population has doubled with Frome becoming a dormitory town for Bristol and Bath. I wonder though, how useful the Frome to Bristol branch line would be right now.

PART TWO

Bill Swaine in Willow Vale, c1933.

Notes from my Father

Every book that touches on family history advises that you should ask the older members of the family about their knowledge of the family history, and details of the life that surrounded them in their early days.

I had done this with my father a few years ago to set up our family tree. I thought that it was now time to extended that to become more involved and find out about what went on in Frome in the early part of the Twentieth Century. In fact I wanted to set up a historical document which would be of interest to all who have a fascination in the past. This would be based on the words of my father and tap his vast memory.

We could find out some those nearly forgotten comings and goings of life in Frome, and especially about the Swaine family living in that unique location at The Bridge, Frome.

My interviews with Bill Swaine took place in 2001 at his home in London.

My questions and remarks are in italics.

William H.S. Swaine, born Frome 1st.May 1913.

Early Days

Firstly, can you tell me a little about where the family were at the time of your birth?

The immediate background before my birth was that my mother and father had married in 1907, and had subsequently rented a house at West End where my sister Mary was born. They had then moved to Catherine Hill House where they lived until 1915, and this was where I was born.

It was 1915 when my grandfather died; he had had many problems, not the least with alcohol, and caused the family much concern. My father had been running the tailoring business for some years, and so after my grandfather's death we moved to The Bridge, and lived 'over the shop.'

Your father was in the fire service before and after his marriage, we see him appearing in several photos in various parades.

Father (J.F.Swaine), was a Lieutenant in the Frome Volunteer Fire Brigade, a position he was very proud of. Their move from West End to Catherine Hill brought him closer to the Fire Station. But the move down to The Bridge was taking him away again, and this would make his 'being on call' much more difficult. I would think that this would have been the time when began to think of leaving the service.

Did he talk of any of his activities in the fire service?

Yes, once they had to go to Stourton House in 1902 to back up the local Fire Brigade when Stourton House was on fire, and they had to stay overnight. The Brigade were very competitive and had won many awards for drills and parades. They once went to Crystal Palace in London to attend a drill championship, and we have a photograph of that. It shows them with a horse drawn appliance, and thus dates it to Edwardian times. I do know that in my childhood, after the war, they had a motorised fire engine.

He did claim that in his younger days, when the fire siren sounded he could be out of bed, get dressed, and be up to the fire station (via Shepherds Barton) in 6 minutes. That was from The Bridge of course, and before he was married. The family had two properties there, numbers 5 and 6.

I have had handed down to me an inscribed barometer which was presented to him by his fire colleagues at the time of their marriage.

Yes, he was married in 1907, and they always had that barometer on display in their home.

What happened to your father during the first war?

Dad was not called up because he became a military tailor, making uniforms and supplying other military items. He did though, have to attend drills at the Keyford Drill Hall towards the end of the war. He would only have been called up in such times as an invasion.

Your grandfather who died in 1915 and left a widow, Jane, did she stay on and live with you?

No, she went next door to stay with my aunt next door at No.5.

This was your father's sister Helen?

Yes, Helen had married Douglas Neale, but he went to the Boer War and never returned. The recording of the activities of military personnel in those days was very poor, and she never got any information from anybody about what happened to him. She was running the ladies clothes shop at No. 5 and taking in her mother was quite a strain for her. She was, by that time a very mobile woman and drove a car, which was quite rare for a woman in those days. She was also getting a social life together, and liked to go off to Bournemouth, so having her mother to live with was quite a burden for her. Somebody once wrote to her and miss-spelt her name as Peale, and it caught on as a nickname, so forever after that she was called Peale.

Earlier Kelly's Directory entries do confirm that the Swaines owned both properties. The tailors were always at No.6 but No.5 was noted as a women's clothing and fancy repository, and run by 2 Misses Swaines. When did Aunt Peale take over?

I'm not sure, but it would have been a few years before the war that she had it all to herself.

Did you have electric light at The Bridge in the twenties?

We had electric light, in the shop, and in the downstairs workroom, and also in the kitchen. We also had it in the first floor sitting room and bedroom. But there was gas only on the second floor. They were not good gas lamps with mantles, but only a piece of pipe coming out of the wall, which turned up and had a naked flame. It did have a little shade on it, but there was one occasion when a curtain blew onto the gas flame and caught fire.

There was a timber structure built at the back; it wasn't built in the 20th Century was it?

Oh no, it was much earlier than that, it would have been built in my grandfather's time, probably the 1870's when they expanded and needed more space for the workpeople. It was a very odd structure with 2 floors built on stilts. The men went to the upper level and had to climb a ladder to get up there.

The staff in the extension, did they have electricity?

The ladies had electricity, but upstairs in the workmen's part, they just had one of these gas pipes. This one came up from the floor and stood about 20 inches from the floor. Again this just had a naked flame.

That was for lighting was it?

Yes, but they didn't need much lighting up there because there was plenty of window space, but yes it was for lighting. I presume they worked until six o'clock in the winter, and obviously needed some light then.

Sounds a bit dangerous doesn't it, but I don't suppose it was in reality.

Don't forget that the men were sitting on the floor of the upper level. They sat with their legs crossed because there were no chairs. They sewed the garments and then passed them through a trap door in the floor to the ladies below. The ladies then did the finishing, stitching, buttonholes etc. Most of the time that I was around, there were 4 men upstairs, two sitting with their backs towards the house, and another two in the wider part at the end, who sat facing one another. There were times when they had more than 4 workmen. When it was built, there may have been six working in there.

Looking at the plan, the men went up the ladder to get to their level.

Yes, it was a wide wooden ladder, and at the top, in an alcove, there was a coke-fired boiler where they heated the irons.

Unlike the ladies, the men were not allowed to use the house facilities, they had to look after themselves for refreshments, and they also had to go down to the river where there was a toilet over-hanging the river.

Did you tell me that there was a father and daughter working there?

Yes, in the twenties there was a man named Lindsay who worked upstairs, his daughter worked downstairs in the extension. They lived in a cottage beside the railway at Spring Gardens. Lindsay was a keen naturalist, and he taught me much about the subject. He knew all the birds and nesting places on his way to work. He pointed out that as well as Kingfishers on the river, there were Dippers nesting under the waterfall at Welshmill.

Who else worked for them?

They had a chap called Willy, a simple fellow who was the 'dogs-body.' His work took in the shop and the house. He did shoe clean-ing, peeled potatoes, delivered parcels, and not least kept the fires going, especially the workmen's boiler for their irons. He would have to bring the coke up from the cellar and up the ladder.

What was the river like in those days?

It was faster flowing and much rubbish got thrown into it at the back there. There were tin cans, which came from No.4, and I dare-say we threw things in as well.

No.4 was the music shop?

Yes, it was owned by Mr Moore who sold gramophone records, sheet music and he also tuned pianos. I think this was where he would have made most of his money.

The music shop later became Woodmancy's didn't it, selling radios and televisions?

There was a Woodmancy the other side of the Market Place in my time, and he obviously took over Mr Moore's shop later on.

What sort of music did the young people like?

Most of the music came from America. Much of it in the early thirties was film music. My uncle visited from Australia occasionally, and once gave my mother some records as a present. These were from the Nuns Chorus.

When I was a schoolboy we had a radio and gramophone con-sole. This was in the late twenties, and the favourite with the young people were portable gramophones.

Go through the names of the businesses occupying The Bridge in your young days.

Starting at the Market Place corner, there was Waters Provisions and Wine Merchant, who later sold out to the International Stores group. Next came the Bridge Hotel, and then there was Mr Moore with the piano and music shop. Next to that was our aunt, Mrs Neale, then Swaines the tailors, and then there was Miss Watts, who had the shop which had that little yard at the back, she sold fancy goods. Next to her was Thick the jeweller, who subsequently sold out to a Mr White. Lastly there was Horsey and Witcomb, the hardware shop who had the brush hanging outside.

The Working Business

As you told me before the men from the workshop were not allowed into the house?

They certainly never went upstairs like the ladies. No doubt from time to time they came through to the back of the shop to the cutting area. My father did the entire first cutting at the back of the shop.

The shop was elegantly fitted, with a mahogany counter, which had drawers underneath. Behind the counter where my father stood there were shelves for rolls of cloth. He had quite a stock of these, which he could show to the customers. There was also a curtained off area beside the front door where the customers could try on clothes.

Where did he get his stock from - Bristol or London?

One regular order came from Leeds, Hare & Co, and I remember that he got some cloth from Selkirk in the lowlands of Scotland. They were delivered from the railway by a GWR horse van, with the cloth wrapped in heavy paper and sometimes in sackcloth. My father always gave the horse an apple.

Did he ever go to Bristol for cloth?

Yes, he went to Bristol, and my mother regularly went to buy for him, she would go off on her own by train. Thursday was early closing day and they would often both go off then. There was a big wholesaler in Bristol called Baker & Baker, and they had a big building with part of it used as a department store. In there they had these little wires going all around the store to carry the money to the cashier. At the back was a big warehouse for the wholesale trade.

This may be where he took me once in the fifties to buy some cloth for my trousers because I remember the wires.

No, it couldn't have been there because it was all blitzed, I think that they re-opened somewhere at the top of Park Street.

Would your parents ever take you?

Oh yes, my mother would take me when I was home from school. It would be my treat and I got a penny bar of Nestles chocolate from the slot machine on Frome station. After she had done her trading in Bristol we would have lunch at the Priory tea rooms at the Tramway Centre, which looked out over the dock. Then in the afternoon we went for a tram ride either down past the Cathedral towards the Clifton Bridge, or for a high level ride up to Durdham Down, which was on the other side of Clifton. This was mainly in the summer, on the open topped trams. One other time we went out towards Filton. That was one of the less attractive rides going up near the prison, and to where the aircraft factory had its ever-expanding works. Another choice was to go the other way towards Bedminster near the Wills cigarette factory.

The big attraction for going on a tram was that they were open topped, and all buses at that time (It was the early twenties) were single-deckers. It was a great thrill to go for a ride on the upper deck, weather permitting of course.

Did your mother help out in the shop, and do any serving?

Not really, she did much of the buying from Bristol, and she got involved at one time with selling some fur items, not coats but collars, muffs, wraps etc. But some of these were stolen, and that just about ended it all. You have to consider that where the average suit may have cost five or six pounds, a fur wrap may have been twenty or twenty-five, and so a theft would be very costly to the business.

My mother would have served in the shop occasionally just to help out.

What went on in the cellar of the house?

My grandfather was a very keen carpenter and he had his workshop down there. He also was an alcoholic, which in the end became his downfall. The cellar was his little hideaway where he would disappear and hide his bottles. Obviously this was before my time, but it had left a profound effect on the family. He had many traumas during in his life, not the least being that at least one of their children had died in infancy, and six of his brothers and sisters had died under the age of 19, mostly of TB.

My aunt was always warning me about drinking being a hereditary thing and that I must keep away from it.

In the cellar he had assembled a tremendous range of tools, but eventually they all became rusted because of the floodwater. We must not forget that from the time my grandfather died until I was 8 years old, floodwater came into the cellars almost every year.

82

After my father took over he never tidied the place up. All sorts of workbenches were down there, and all the tools were in racks on the wall, and there was also a lathe. In the end it was such a shambles, all the metalwork had turned black and the timber had rotted. I am sure that my father was very disgusted with the set up that his father had, and subsequently had left it alone. It would have stayed untouched until they moved out in 1936.

The situation obviously had an extreme effect on your father, because he completely stayed off drink, or never even went in a pub.

It certainly did, and must have affected the business. My father did smoke though.

Did he ever grow his own tobacco in your time in his garden at Waterloo?

No, he always smoked 'Sunripe' ready-made cigarettes. I don't know what sort of cigarette cards were in those packets, but certainly he never used 'roll your own' cigarettes, or grew his own tobacco as he did later on.

He used to row his boat down to the garden; did you ever go with him?

Yes, and I would sometimes row myself, it was quite fun to take the rowing boat off the landing stage and row it up the river. My father sometimes walked to the garden, he would go up through the market yard and up on to the railway line, and cut across the railway bridge. Then he could drop down and cross into the garden from there.

He could obviously row down there in about three or four minutes, but it must have taken him seven or eight if he walked.

Yes, but he could collect watercress from beside the railway line, so that was one of his reasons for walking. In the late summer he brought boxes and boxes of apples back from the garden by boat. He would store them in the box rooms at the top of the house, and there was this forever smell of rotting apples up there.

Whatever else happened with your grandfather, he gave your father the best possible training for tailoring, because he sent him to serve his apprenticeship at Savile Row.

My father had a story, that at one time while he was at Savile Row, somebody called them all out into Regent Street to see a motorcar, which was coming along. They all went out to have a look, and there was a man with a red flag walking in front of it.

That dates it to before 1896, when the red flag law was repealed.

Church

Who was the most religious in that household?
My father I would say, but as he got older his interest declined.

In my young days I was strictly brought up, God-fearing Church of England. As a 5-year-old I had to say my prayers. My father was quite strict when I was very young.

Your grandmother was a Bible reader wasn't she?
She was Baptist, and my father was brought up as Baptist. My parents married at Lympsham Church, which is Church of England. That is between Weston and Burnham, in north Somerset and was my mother's family's area. My aunt Blanche was an organist at the church for their wedding.

When my sister Mary wanted to be married in Frome, the vicar of St John's Church would not marry them because my family were non-conformists. I did not understand this, because from the time I was seven we all went to St John's every Sunday, and I went to the Sunday School. Because of the family history of non-conformists he wouldn't be persuaded to conduct the marriage. At Holy Trinity church they were not so strict and the marriage was performed there. My father was also a sidesman at St Johns, and for a time I was a coat boy, so I could never understand the vicar's decision.

I had sometimes gone with my grandmother to the Baptist Church, which is almost next door to Catherine Hill House where I was born. Also I used to enjoy the service occasionally at Zion church in Cork Street. I went there with my friend John Vincent and his father, which didn't please my parents much.

I remember that at the end of every service the minister would announce how much money was collected. On one occasion John Vincent had put a farthing in the collection to see if the minister would announce it, but he didn't. He was always a bit of a scamp was John. My cousin Catherine Trotman went to that church as well. Not at that time though, because she was then living in London.

There are various odd little churches in the Trinity area, aren't there?
There was a primitive Methodist, and not far away was the Baptist church, and there is also the South Parade church.

The Business

You mentioned that in the shop your father had mahogany furniture and fittings. In the back shop there was his cutting table, and what else?

Above that fireplace, there was a glass frame with reproductions of all the medal ribbons of the army, I wish we had kept it because it was very interesting. Medal ribbons were one of the military lines which he sold.

You told me that he never got called up for military service?

No, because he was a military tailor, he was a supplier and local tailor for the army, and had drawers full of army paraphernalia. He sold puttees, medal ribbons, rank insignia - chevrons and officer's pips, and other such things. The army had quite a presence in the area with the Warminster garrison being close by, and many hundreds of soldiers were billeted in the town. His workmen too would have been exempt from a call up. It was a very busy time for them. I was only five when the war ended so what I can remember is very limited.

It seems that your father carried on with the fire service for a while after moving back to The Bridge in 1915?

Yes, I think for a short while, but he was running the business by himself, so I don't think that he carried on for long.

He was also a Councillor, we have a photo of him with the Australian Ambassador at the Recreation Ground, which we think was after the war. He must have been quite proud to be contributing to both the fire service and the local council.

The death of his father would have meant that his commitment as a councillor could not be the same, so as well as giving up the fire service, the civic duties had to go as well.

Did he make any ladies clothes?

Yes, in a small way, but not generally speaking. I recall that he had some elegant fashion plates, and some of the advertising showed some ladies clothing.

Were there any other very busy times?

The busiest time my father had was when somebody died. Following a death, the bereaved family wanted to be dressed in black, and he got the mourning orders. All the work people usually had to be called in to work over a weekend or whenever, and get the clothing finished in time for the funeral.

Had you ever had any thoughts of being trained for the business?

Although I could just about work a sewing machine, I was never any good at needlework or handy-work. My aspirations always were different, and so there were never any thought of me going into the business. Also, by the time I had left school Burtons were coming into the town. Ready-made fifty-shilling suits were affecting the trade. My father had to charge twice that price. It was also in the depression and people didn't pay their bills. A leading auctioneer in Frome defaulted on my father for quite a big bill, but my father would never go to court. Apparently it was not the done thing in a small town for one trader to sue another, but it wasn't right as far as my father was concerned. Many people defaulted and this put him under pressure.

I suppose that in 99% of his life, he had no problems?

He was fined once, £60 a good deal of money in those days. He had neglected to stamp his workmen's National Health cards for the 9d or 1/6 a week or whatever it was. They prosecuted him for not keeping up these payments. The day after he had attended the court one of the attending magistrates came in the shop and paid my father's outstanding bill, he too had been behind.

He must have been quite a proud man, and highly skilled. At functions, people would be wearing the clothes he had made. The shop would have sold a good deal of sundries and small items, such as needles and cottons. What else would you buy from the shop?

Leggings were a stock item. Farmers wore smart leather leggings over their boots. When he packed up he had many of those left over. There was a very limited stock of anything ready-made which he kept. Nowadays you can get suits off the peg in all sizes, but in those days it wasn't like that.

Did you ever have a made-to-measure suit?

No, but I had two suits which were not collected by a customer, one was a brown tweed and the other a navy suit, I had these at the time I first came to London.

He made those, did he?

My father made them, but obviously they were not intended for
me. They were made for this customer who defaulted, the person
paid a deposit for both but never came back, and so I had them. The
chap was from out of town I think, certainly not a local.

***What age were you when you had your first pair of long trou-
sers?***

*I ask this because he made me my first pair when I was thirteen,
and we went to Bristol by train to get the cloth. I mentioned this
before, when we went to this big store and warehouse, and they all
knew him as Mr Swaine of Frome.*

I remember a photograph of myself playing cricket in the market yard with a Sexey's cap, I had a blazer on as well, also long white
trousers. I would have thought that I was about thirteen.

How was the shop partitioned?

There was a rail with clothes hanging on that effectively screened
off an alcove at the front to make it private. Any major fitting would
have been done at the back of the shop. There was a wooden screen,
which separated the front part of the shop with the cutting area behind. This had glass above and was in mahogany to match the rest
of the fittings.

What do you remember about the kitchen in the back?

This was the main kitchen for the house, and being on the ground
floor my mother would entertain there. Visitors came in for a cup of
tea and a chat, and for main meals all the food had to be carried upstairs to the dining table. The kitchen was my mother's domain, and
she did all the cooking.

Would there have been a gas cooker, or range?

I'm sure she had a gas stove, and I think there was a coal oven as
well, most people had a range.

***On the first floor there was a front sitting room and a back sit-
ting room. Was that because your family split into two groups?***

The back sitting room was seldom used. A little at Christmas,
but it was always the front dining and sitting room, which was the
family room. The back room was rather small and genteel in it's fur-
nishing, I don't remember sitting in there. In the front room we had
a big sofa, two armchairs and a big dining table with 6 or 8 chairs

88

around it. There was a sideboard and a piano - my sister liked to play this. We had our big evening meal in there, which was supper at 8 o'clock, this gave my father a couple of hours after closing time to do a few things, or go to the garden.

Also on the second floor there was a big cupboard at the top of the stairs. In this there was a big tailors dummy, and also there were two or three flags on poles. These would be hung out of the upstairs windows on special days and holidays. I always remember he had a yellow Scottish flag as well as a Union Jack. Why he had the Scottish flag I don't know.

Your father had a fretwork machine in the fifties, did he have that then?

He had that, and kept it at the end of the ladies workroom in the extension. He kept it near the doorway and he did use it at times.

I asked this because it was made by 'Hobbies' who had a their shop in New Oxford Street close to where we lived in London. He must have bought it by mail order from their catalogue. He later gave it to me and I took it home.

Hobbies also produced a journal called Hobbies Weekly, or something like that. My father took pictures from calendars, which he then stuck on pieces of plywood and made jigsaw puzzles.

I remember these, because the pieces were never interlocking. When I had the machine I made a point of making jigsaws with the pieces interlocking.

Are you interested in jigsaw puzzles?

No, but I once made one from a picture of the Golden Arrow train coming out of Victoria Station and passing the BOAC building.

Christmas / School / Trips away

What was Christmas like in Frome?

Instead of hanging up stockings we hung up pillowcases. One Christmas I wanted a Hornby train-set but I didn't get one. I got a different make, and this didn't impress me at all. I must have let this be known because the following Christmas I got the real thing, which had a LNER engine. It was fine except the front bogie wheels of the engine kept coming off the tracks, later they made these without bogies and they ran much better. We also had a folding bagatelle table, which would be set up at Christmas and be very popular.

Who were the residents at No.6 long term?

Grandmother had moved into No. 5 after my grandfather's death in 1915, so it was just the family only. My mother's family lived near Highbridge, but later they had moved to Frome. The grandfather moved to The Bridge when he was ailing and died there. Obviously Peale and Grandmother Jane came in occasionally, and we also went into their house.

Tell me about your schooling.

When I was 7, I went as a weekly boarder to Clifford School in Beckington. That was where I first got friendly with John Vincent. At 11, I went from there to Sexey's School at Bruton, as a weekly boarder. This was until I was 17, when I went to London. Hence my Frome activities were generally confined to weekends and holidays.

I had three main friends through my school days, John Vincent from the age of 7 became a friend for life. He was the son of Harry Vincent, the jeweller from Cheap Street. Then there was Bertie Champion who was the son of the manager of the malt house beside the station. They lived in Portway in one of those houses that faced the high pavement. His mother died while he was young, and he and his father always then came to us for Christmas dinner. At other times we would go to their house and listen to the cup final or boat race on their radio. The early days of radio were very exciting for us, especially when we could listen to a major event.

The other friend I had was Jack Seward, son of the Frome builder. I also got on well with Arthur Sutton, who was a dayboy at Bruton, but he was in the year ahead of me. Sutton's father had a furniture business in the Market Place, on the site where Woolworth's now have their store. They sold good quality furniture and upholstery. Two of his son's became choristers and went to public schools. Arthur though didn't, he was the eldest and had the same education as me at Bruton.

What was Sexeys like?

Fairly small, but not particularly strict. Firstly I boarded in the town, but then later moved to Cliffe House, which was near the school. Only about 30% of the pupils were boarders. Many of the day-boys came from Evercreech and travelled on the Somerset and Dorset Railway, which was nearby. Quite a few cycled in from various places including Frome and Castle Cary.

When I was at Cliffe House I wrote to the Daimler Car Company and asked for a catalogue. Much to my embarrassment a salesman turned up with a car from Bristol. Everybody had a good laugh about that, and I had my leg pulled, the company were obviously impressed with the address.

That other school in Bruton has an awesome appearance, which is that?

Kings, which was an expensive boys school, and was more for the sons of gentlemen and professional people. It had its own chapel and very fine sports ground. The two schools didn't mix much at that time, but I have seen now that Sexey's School have played against Kings at cricket. That is something that they never did in my day.

Did anyone famous go to those schools?

C.C.C. Case who played for Somerset went to Kings. He later had a little sports car and drove me from Frome to watch Somerset play against Yorkshire at Bath. That was when I was 15 and he was playing for Somerset that day. He said to me, 'I don't mind how slow I make my runs so long as I don't get out.' He then took about 2 hours to make 19 runs.

He had though, made a number of centuries for Somerset. I once batted with him for Frome Cricket Club when I was 17, against the firm of Stother & Pitt of Bath. He was very pleased, because I was last but one man in, and stayed to make 3 or 4 not out while he completed his century. His family had a leather tanning business in Frome.

Which school did your sister Mary, go to?

Bruton, but not the one I went to which was Sexeys, she went to Sunny Hill School. This is half a mile further up the road from Sexeys, and she also was a weekly boarder. My father would walk to the station with her each Monday morning, and they walked very fast. He said that they walked up there in 8 minutes, which is very fast going. Sunny Hill School has got a different name now, but it was a very well-to-do school.

I expect that you and John Vincent were quite a pair of lads, what did you get up to?

All sorts of things, one of the hobbies of that time was collecting bird's eggs. I do recall that on one occasion John put an egg into a boot hanging outside a shoe shop in Stony Street. We then made a smart departure.

Did the family go on any trips in the twenties?

When I was a seven-year-old, my mother hired a horse and carriage to take us to Longleat via Woodlands. There were two horses so we got along quite well, we had the two grandmothers with us. I think that the charge for the carriage and pair was 3/6d.

Another time my mother, sister and myself went on an open motor coach. There was a photograph of this, and I was wearing my felt hat from the preparatory school. The coach, or charabanc as it was called in those days, came from Bristol, and it had a pale blue open hood. The trip was the Cheapstreet tradesman's annual outing to Bournemouth, and the photograph was taken in Bournemouth close to the pier. We went on an invitation from John Vincent's father. Some of those early charabancs had solid tyres, but I think that this was towards the late twenties when we could enjoy a ride on pneumatic tyres.

Some of the early buses must have had solid tyres. Do you remember those?

The first Bath bus to Frome had solid tyres, and I think that the first Warminster buses also had them. By the time the Bath and Bristol companies took over the routes, advancements had been made and these would have had the comfort of inflated tyres.

I know that when I stayed at The Bridge the sounds of the different motor engines were very distinct. It seemed to echo a bit and you could just sit there, or wake up in the morning and listen to all the very distinctive engine sounds that went by. Even the sound of a dog barking was very crisp and clear. Being a boy from London, this was one of the things that I particularly noticed, against the muffled sounds of the big city. Do you remember any other motor vehicles?

I remember that when I was at school at Beckington in the late evening a procession of something like 20 motor coaches went through going back to Bristol from Bournemouth. These were the open topped type, and they passed by about nine o'clock in the evening all with their hoods down. That was a works outing from one of the big factories of Bristol, Wills tobacco or someone like that.

Then at Frome in the twenties, each Good Friday, there was a rally of motorcycles from Slough going to Devon. They all went one after the other down North Parade and then noisily over the Bridge as they revved up for the climb up Bath Street. This was about 6 am, and we would get up and watch them.

Are there any other trips that you can recall?

My parents hired a taxi to take us to a Christmas party at Kay Lawson's house. Her father was manager of Cockey's Factory, and he lived quite a big house in Westbury Leigh. For two years running we went there, and I was quite struck coming home when we saw the little spotted electric lights of Frome twinkling in the distance. This was from the top of the hill outside Chapmanslade, and I had never been out like that before at night.

There was the time when my father and T.T.N. Biss won the Somerset pairs bowls championship. The final was played in Bristol and we went to that. Afterwards we went to the Priory restaurant where the trophy, a big rose bowl, was in the middle of the table. Everyone was making quite a fuss of the pair of them. Biss was an art metal dealer who had a workshop in Apple Alley. That is at the back of Cheap Street.

After having won the championship of Somerset, they were eligible for the national championship in London. The finals then were played at Bellingham, but I don't think that they made too much progress in the competition.

Remind us about some of those long forgotten smells that would have been around the town.

The bakers in Palmer Street on the high pavement, always had the aroma of freshly baked bread, this was always very pleasant. And there was the malt smells from the Malt house up by the railway, which combined with the steam and coal in the goods yard. There was brewing from both the Lamb and United breweries, and all the horsey smells that were always around. The blacksmith up in Christchurch Street was always busy, with his business providing sound and smells. The cattle market was full of all the pungent smells of manure, and that was on the streets too, especially when animals came by 'on the hoof.'

One area to avoid was out at Spring Gardens. There you not only had to cope with the smells of the gas works, but the open sewage works were prominent with their odours.

One particularly interesting aroma came from a tar-cart, which provided tar for road repairing. Parents who had children with bronchial problems, took them to inhale the fumes from this tar-heating appliance. It was a popular belief that the fumes would ease their children's breathing problems.

Were there any particularly annoying sounds around?

The one, which comes straight to mind, was a particular instance when I once went to see a film show on a Saturday evening at the The Picture Palace. This was a little cinema close to the bottom of the Church steps at St Johns, and right in the middle of the film the church bells started ringing. They were having a practice session in preparation for the following Sunday. It was most distracting. This cinema was converted from the Mechanic's Institute and showed silent films with the accompaniment of a pianist.

Did the family go to Bath very often?

A couple of times we went there to pantomimes and other times for shopping or for a stroll around the gardens. The journey was always by bus, which only took us as far as the top of the hill at Coombe Down. There we had to change on to one of those lovely little trams that they used to have in Bath.

Frome was always a great place for taking walks, with the fresh air and interesting countryside it couldn't be beaten. Which were your favourites?

I remember, and probably you do too, walks through Spring Gardens to Orchardleigh on Sundays with my father and mother. Another of my favourites is the walk to Rodden Church. That lovely stream and mill there, with the babbling brooks.

I would have been distracted by the railway on that walk.

The church was a mile out of town, but the vicar lived at Rodden Vicarage, which was on the edge of Frome at the bottom of Styles Hill. One of his sons was a famous cricketer. He had this big house, and he would have to follow the footpath across the fields to get to Rodden. When the railway loop line was built in 1933, the foot-bridge was installed across the railway so that he and others could get to the church.

Of course there is now also the by-pass to contend with, but I expect the footpath is still there.

Did you watch much cricket at Frome?

In '29 and '30 I played cricket for Frome. It was a great pity at that time that I did not get more coaching, as this would have made a great difference to me. Of course I watched cricket with my Father later. He would have a rest after lunch and then we would walk up to the ground, and we would sit in front of the old grandstand. The grandstand was built for the annual Cheese Show, which was held every September. There was a time when the Cheese show was held in the field at West End. The organisers cemented pieces of glass into the top of the walls so that people could not climb in without paying.

Talking of cricket. In the mid-twenties when the Frome Cricket Club was founded, my father had an order to supply caps to the club, and they were pink. I don't think that the colour was too popular, because by the time that I played they had changed to blue.

Where was the old rugby ground?

After the first war they re-constituted up at the back of Nunney Road, and I'm sure that is where they played earlier, and is where my father had his photograph taken with the team in 1896.

How about Frome Town Football Club, were they going strong in the twenties?

Yes, we would watch them from time to time. They had a burly centre forward called Wyndham Haynes. I was standing behind the goal on one occasion and one of his shots came right through the back of the net.

He then went to play for Portsmouth and was their all-time record goal-scorer. A very burly chap he was, and I think that his Portsmouth scoring record has recently beaten by a player called Whitingham.

Years later when I was staying in Frome, I was with my cousin and we walked into a pub in Tytherington, which is very near to where the Frome by-pass comes through. Wyndham was the landlord of the pub, and I had a chat with him about the old days. This must have been in the nineteen-sixties, I think.

J.F. Swaine can be seen here in the foreground, acting in his role of Councillor for the visit of a Statesman. The High Commissioner of Australia, was in Frome for the ceremonial planting of a tree in Victoria Park. Probably just after WW1.

The Frome Volunteer Fire Brigade was always proud of its turnout. Their drill displays won them many trophies at functions around the West of England. Here they are showing their prowess at a display at the Crystal Palace, London. This would have been in Edwardian times. Most Fire Brigades became motorised around the period 1920-2.

A typical 'firms' outing in the early days of motoring. The charabanc is about to depart from the Lamb Hotel at the top of Bath Street for a run to the coast. Note the solid tyres and everybody suited in their Sunday 'best.' Postcard by A.E. Whittington.

The Swaine family of Edwardian times, in a photograph which has barely survived. Back row: Margaret, Fred, Janet, Tom. Seated: James Treasure, Jane, Helen.

A little bit of old Frome. At the bottom of the Church steps facing the top of Cheap Street. The Mechanic's Institute can be seen on the left.

The Frome Rugby Football Team 1896

Standing: ____, Happerfield, ____, Yerbury, J.F.Swaine, ____,
A.W.Edwards, ____, Ben Pyle, Clegg, H.T.Cross.
Middle row: ____, H.Hodder, T.H.(Harry) Vincent, Read, Cockey,
L.V.Trotman, Latchem, L.('Masher') Wilkins,
Front row: A.Elton, H.H.Newport, J.E.Batten.

Transport / Traders

Was the bus service very good in Frome?

It was very regular, both to Bath and Trowbridge. I can remember when the Trowbridge bus started, because it was the first time that I had seen an open topped double-decker bus. This must have been about 1922, and also there was a regular service that came from Wells or Glastonbury on its way to London. I sometimes travelled to London on a Royal Blue service, and there was also a coach from Bristol, which came through Frome, bound for Bournemouth.

The bus services, as we knew them, were just getting organised at that time, but earlier there were a privately run little bus services. One of those ran from Warminster through Corsley to Frome, before the Bath bus took over that route.

Did you ever see a steam driven lorry?

Oh yes, a Sentinel with a curved front, and then there was the Foden with a tapered front. I think Frome Council had one of those, and one of the breweries had a Sentinel. Talking of lorries, every fortnight or so, an old chain driven lorry came from Bristol, and picked up any suits that customers wanted to be dry cleaned. I think it was Whiteways Dye Works and Laundry. There were no dry cleaners in Frome at that time.

Bath Street is very steep, did horse drawn carts get up there all right?

I would have thought that sometimes a local horseman would have to lend his big horse to help out for a shilling. Singers had a very small-wheeled horse drawn wagon, which picked up heavy equipment from their factory to take to the station. It needed four horses to pull it up Bath Street.

Mostly horse traffic would go the other way, via King Street, and Vicarage Street, although sometimes these roads would be very congested.

Cattle came down Bath Street on market days 'on the hoof,' and they would have walked a long way. Some would have come from Blatchbridge, and been led up to Keyford and then down Bath Street. Others would have come from Marston or even Nunney. A right mess they often made on the roads, as of course did the horses, but there were always street cleaners around.

How about tradesman's deliveries to the Bridge, what can you remember of those?

There was a milkman who came who had two churns with lids and these were connected to a wooden yoke across his shoulders, he would stop and scoop milk out of these for us. I think that he must have been independent and he came from somewhere up at the top of North Parade. We would go and buy cream on a Sunday morning from Cox's dairy in the middle of Cheap Street. There must have been a wholesaler or farmer who supplied these dairymen. Many other rounds-men delivered around the town including the Mount Pleasant Dairy milkman who supplied lovely milk from his horse drawn cart. Other traders would deliver such as a baker's boy on a bicycle with a big basket at the front.

Were you much of a train enthusiast as a boy?

Yes, I witnessed the trial run of the Great Western Railway 'King George V' locomotive on its first trials in 1926. It stopped for about an hour in the sidings at Rodden Road, and I took a photograph of it, but unfortunately that photo got lost. I was disappointed that the 'King' had a small low sided coal tender, but the Great Western Railway put this right later on, and the great 'Kings and Castles' had high sided tenders like the big engines of the LMS or LNER.

Of course they didn't have the loop line then where the express trains bypassed Frome, all the trains came through Frome Station. I think it was in 1933 that the loop was put in.

There was always a great deal of action around the stretch of line into Frome and around the triangle of lines before Frome station. All the coal traffic that came from Radstock went into the sidings there, and wagons were shunted around making up trains for various destinations. As a boy I was often around there watching the shunting going on. Then we had all the coal trains coming down from the Midlands with the different colliery names on the sides, these went on through the station to the southwest.

Was the Express Dairy milk depot with the tall chimney in operation at that time?

In my youngest days that site was a commercial garden, a form of a nursery. The factory was built sometime in the '20s, and the siding alongside was put in by the Express Dairy to take milk wagons by train mostly up to the Cricklewood depot in London. Lorries would come from the farms and unload the churns into the factory where the milk would be pasteurised before being dispatched in bulk.

There were those mills around the Wallbridge area, they must have been in full flow.

They employed so many people, that in the early morning and again in the evening, there would be a wave of factory workers walking down Christchurch Street and Portway from the artisan's houses on the other side of town. Others would have come in by bicycle from the villages. Only one factory was there, Tuckers, but it was split into two sections, sometimes you would see bales of wool being off-loaded from a lorry and being pushed across the road to the other side.

This flow of workmen coming to and from factories is now seen less and less, but in your day it would have been part of life.

Nowadays they wouldn't walk, people would travel by car.

I can remember the Wallbridge factory blaring out the radio programme 'Music While You Work' in the fifties, this was only on for about a quarter of an hour in the mornings and afternoons, but was a well-liked musical interlude.

Have you any other memories of workmen travelling about?

There was an occasion when I was travelling to London by train and leaving Frome in the early morning, when there was quite a cluster of men travelling off to Melksham to work at the Avon Rubber factory. Others were going off to work at the woollen mills in Trowbridge, and all having the benefit of cheap rate workmen tickets that were available in those days for early morning travel to work.

Tell me a bit about the Cockey's firm, they made all those lovely little ornate lampposts.

Cockey's I don't know too much about. The chief thing for them in my day was making gasholders, and containers for agricultural use. Their factory was by the triangle of railway lines near the station. You could hear the banging of metal from The Bridge sometimes if the wind was in the right direction.

As well as the little lampposts, they did also supply about a dozen big lampposts that were placed around the town in the early 1900's, these were at the time that electricity replaced gas.

A factory you haven't asked me about is the silk mill. They had extensive buildings behind the vicarage in Vicarage Street. I went over them once with Jack Seward the builder's son. I did three different visits with him to projects that they worked on, one was going over the silk mills, another was to go around the electric light works, and the third was to see the re-building of Mells House. This was the mansion being re-built for Sir Reginald McKenna, who was chairman of the Midland Bank.

Going to School / Holidays

You went to school in Bruton, which was situated near the Somerset & Dorset Railway, what were your recollections of this line?

It was never as well thought of before as it has been since it closed. It always seemed to be the poor relation of the Great Western Railway, and was slow and had old stock. I had probably only travelled on it about three times. One of these was for a family holiday to Bournemouth in about 1921, when we went by Great Western to Radstock and changed to the S&D. We had a very smoky climb up over the Mendips, and eventually got to Bournemouth West. There we switched to one of the very luxurious taxicabs that the town had at that time. They had well-padded seats and a pleasure to ride in. My father actually bought a rowing boat on the beach at Bournemouth while we were there, and had it sent back by the Somerset and Dorset Railway. I think that this boat lasted him right through until they moved.

On another occasion, when I was staying with an aunt on the Somerset Levels between Cheddar and Bridgwater, a group of us went from Westhay Shapwick to Burnham-on-sea on the S&D. The station at Burnham was covered like a shed, and had only a single line and one platform. The railway came out of it at the other end and went down to the quay, where coal was shipped over from South Wales and was transferred directly onto railway trucks.

The third occasion that I travelled on the Somerset and Dorset was when I went to play school football at Street. I was a weekly boarder and we went from the local station, which was Cole, and changed at Evercreech Junction for Glastonbury. We did not have any sentiment for steam trains then, they were just functional. I seem to remember that I went back to Frome via Wells. Cole station was within walking distance of the school and was used by the school.

Since it's closure, the Somerset & Dorset Railway is much talked about and well regarded and it has almost cult status.

It was certainly thought by us as the poor relation, especially as it had been partly taken over by the Midland Railway in 1922, and had dirty black engines most of the time. It was only in its later days that they had put modern engines on the trains. One of these headed the Pines Express, their most prestigious train, which came down from the north to Bath, and then on to Bournemouth.

That time we went to Bournemouth, my father had to keep the shop open on a Saturday, and he followed on in the evening travelling via Westbury and Salisbury. We stayed at the Woodley Towers Hotel, which has now been pulled down to make way for the Conference Centre. It was very exciting to wake up and look out at the pier and sea.

All the Swaines seemed to go to Bournemouth, we went there by coach a few times in my day.

The popular place for most Frome families was Weymouth for holidays. It was a bit cheaper than Bournemouth and it was on a direct line. We often went there but that was only for day trips. Another time we went by train was when we had a holiday in Torquay. I lost a coat and my mother was furious.

Did you ever go out in Aunt Peale's car, the 3 wheeler?

Many times, quite often she took me to school in Beckington. If she took me out at the same time as my grandmother, I used to sit on the hood at the back, safety was not much of a consideration then. Sometimes when we were coming back from Beckington, and coming to the top of Old Ford Hill, Aunt would hiss at some young women standing beside the roadside. Apparently they were staff from the Blue House, who were trying to supplement their income by picking up male travellers.

She too went to Bournemouth in that little car. I think that she must have had some social life there because she would never take me. She was friendly with the Sewards and they stayed at the Manchester Hotel in Bournemouth, which I think is still there.

She had an accident on one occasion coming home, when a tyre burst, and that is not good news on a three-wheeler. She went off the road at a place called Pepperbox Hill and ended up in Salisbury Hospital. The make of the car was a New Hudson, and before that she had a 4-wheeled car, but this only had 2 seats. I do remember that it had a registration DP 1 because I used to study those numbers as a boy, and that one came from Reading.

Twice when my uncle and Aunt Margaret came from Australia for a holiday in England, they bought a car. When they went back Aunt Peale bought it from them, one was a massive Buick, an American car, and this was most unusual for her. The other was a Morris Oxford 4-seater and she drove me to cricket at Southampton. This was one of the hottest days I have ever known, and we parked inside the ground and sat on the burning hot roof of the car to watch the cricket.

Where did she park her car in Frome?

She shared a garage in Grant's yard, which is at the end of King Street. There was a yard, which the builders, decorator and sign writers shared. The headmaster of Christchurch School also parked there, he had an MG car.

Very few people used taxis in those days, there are very long taxi ranks now outside the shopping centre in Cork Street. I don't suppose that in previous times a working man in Frome had ever hired a taxi. There were Cox's Taxis in Church Street, and Mino's at Badcox next to Bertwhistles fish and chip shop. There would have been one or two taxis on the rank outside the station, black rickety looking things. Then there was the taxi-man Martin, who also had a van. He moved our furniture from Frome to London in 1947, when we returned after the war.

Are there any parts of Frome that you don't know?

Yes, there are parts of Frome that I didn't know at all well. Over The Butts and down beyond where Crown Tours had their garage, and also the area of Lower Keyford. All the higher areas of Frome were less travelled by us, except to the park of course. There was also the area behind Somerset Road where the workhouse and the Isolation Hospital were located. I didn't see much of these, no doubt small towns have no need for an isolation hospital any more. Scarlet fever was a scourge then.

Was the Workhouse the first asylum?

I think that it was built as a home for old men and young boys, but it wasn't the asylum as such, that was the building that looked similar to the Blue House at Keyford.

Did your father ever have any rivals in the town?

There was a tailor who set up in the Market Place called Willis in my younger days, who was also a bespoke tailor. He didn't produce my father's quality of work, and would annoy my father by coming into his shop every now and again to buy some lining or silk or little things. If one tradesman approached another tradesman in a similar business, they would let him have something at cost price.

Was there much trade for small objects?

My father didn't sell ties, but he might have had a pair of braces or two, because if people were buying a suit they may want braces. Sometimes when someone spent something and there was an odd halfpenny or a farthing for change, he would give them a small clip of safety pins instead of a coin.

We have talked about the neighbours, did you ever know Mr Thick?

Thick had a very nice jewellery shop two doors down. Herbert White who took over from him, later moved the business into Cheap Street. Horsey and Witcomb of course had the hardware shop at the end of the terrace.

I was always fascinated by some power tools that they had in their window in the fifties. There was a Wolf drill, and a Bridges hand drill attached to a lathe, which I always fancied.

What went on at the Lit Club in Frome?

It was a library, and to an extent a commercial building. But from the time I was a youngster it was a reading room and billiard club, with also a card room. The caretaker who ran it was also secretary of Frome Town Football Club, and he got a life suspension for playing an illegal player. It was a player that he had brought in and paid ten shillings a match to play. This was strictly against the rules because it was all completely amateur in those days.

Did you ever go to the Market Hall, which was where your mother had her photo taken in fancy dress?

The Market Hall was a factory in my time, but before the first war it would have been what was the equivalent of the Grand Theatre.

My Aunt Jan who later emigrated to Australia, appeared in Gilbert and Sullivan there, and I presume also that they had dances and other functions. After the war, the Grand became a war memorial hall and the Market Hall was less used for functions. We went to see a production of Gilbert and Sullivan, and also the Grand held Christmas fairs and similar functions.

It wasn't commercially economical, and the building soon became a cinema. When it was turned into a cinema there was a stipulation that it should also be available to the Frome Operatic Society.

Relations / London

Catherine Trotman, your cousin, was always close to your family. Her mother was a Rawlings, and both names were prominent business families in Frome at the height of the industrial times.

Also my grandmother was a Rawlings, and that is where the families connect. Rawlings were cardmakers to the woollen industry, and the Trotmans were brewers. Both families have very well documented family histories, with ancestry going back to the 12th Century.

What did your sister Mary do when she left school?

She went into nursing at the Cheltenham Hospital children's department. We motored to see her occasionally in Aunt Peale's car, going via Chippenham and Malmesbury. Mary was a little unhappy at first at having to do many of the menial tasks that were given to a junior in a hospital, but she became a very proficient nurse. After Cheltenham she moved to Bristol for a while, and shocked me by telling me how much poverty there was there. She was a maternity nurse, and was visiting patient's homes. When she married and lived in Hereford she became a Sister, and later became assistant Matron during the war.

So when Mary left home at 17 she never came back. This applies to you also because 3 years later you must have left for London?

Mary was married from home, I told you about that previously when the vicar at St John's refused to perform the ceremony. That would have been about 1936, a year before I was married.

Interestingly, when we travelled down for their wedding in Frome, we travelled via Bath. On the return journey, we had some confetti on our clothes, and a ticket collector thought we were newly married and showed us into a First Class compartment and locked us in. The lovely brown armchair seats in First Class really impressed me.

Do you remember when you first took my mother to Frome to meet your folks, because mum had vivid memories of that moment and was quite struck by going in and seeing the grandmother sitting in a corner wearing a bonnet.

110

I don't remember it too well, it would probably have been about 1934 when I was 21. I do remember that we were staying there once and her Polish friends called in on their way to Devon. They were wearing trousers and this really shocked my mother.

We could change direction for a moment at this point and talk about your early life in London. Where were you working?

I was working for Atlas Insurance as an underwriter's clerk at Lloyds. I also played football for them, and we had an occasion when we played a Cup Final at Highbury - Arsenal's ground. The match at Highbury would have been in 1935. I was going steady with Betty then, and she came to the match. We lost 6-2 to the Prudential.

There was a report of the match in the Times, and they said that I showed a good turn of speed on the left wing. Another report in an insurance journal said that we were weak on the wings. Our centre forward traced me a couple of years ago and we had a chat.

Before we went to the ground we had a reception at the Atlas offices. They were in Cheapside on the corner by the Guildhall. They have now amalgamated with someone else, but their trademark was a figure of Atlas holding the world above his head. There is still that symbol over one of the doors to this day. I stayed with that company right through until wartime.

In the thirties the tailoring business was winding down, was it in 1935 that it finally closed?

Later, I'm pretty sure that it was the year that my sister got married, 1936.

So it had run for a century then. What were the pressures on your father at that time?

He had overdrafts by this time, and with no natural future for the business he had let it run down. It was depressed times and people did not pay their bills, he had slowly got into dept. The Westminster Bank forced his hand in the end, and foreclosed on him. The premises including the living accommodation had to be sold.

I told you before that my father was slack about paperwork and he had previously been fined. At this time, he was not opening letters from the banks or solicitors, they were obviously sending all sorts of final demands and he was ignoring them. Probably he could have come to terms with the bank if he had acted differently, but that was how it was.

It was though, a civilised affair, and after the foreclosure and sale, they did have some money left over. My aunt and grandmother had chipped in with some money, as relatives would do, to help them out before the shop closed and that had eased the situation for a while.

What were the options, the family still had the house and shop next door at No. 5?

There was no question of them moving into number 5, Peale ran that shop selling her hats and ladies dresses, and there was also the grandmother living there. My father had rented homes before and he would do it again.

There were 2 desirable residences available that they could choose from, Conigre House or Welsh Mill Lodge which was opposite that little iron suspension bridge that can be seen in their courting photograph.

He was quite a handyman, so he could take on a big house and they chose Conigre House. He also loved going to the sale-rooms, and he picked up quality furniture for a song. My mother was also very business-like and I expect that she took them through that period. They also took in lodgers at Conigre to help pay for the running of the house.

My father did put a sewing machine in one room to carry on doing a bit of tailoring, but I think he only did a small amount after that. He was soon to take a job working in the Fuel Office, and he kept that job on during the war, and right on until he retired in 1952.

Yes I often went to see him at his office at Wallbridge House in the later days. Fuel was rationed and he was supposed to have a reputation for being very 'careful' with the rations during the war.

Of course, when my mother died in 1950, he then moved in with his sister Peale at No. 5 The Bridge. There was a big sale of furniture from Conigre House and Percy Quick of Cooper and Tanner conducted the sale.

I was there for that sale, and was intrigued and horrified by seeing every item with a number on it, and then being systematically sold off.

After this you had more to do with Frome than I did. Since I left home in 1929 I never actually lived in Frome again. During the war I was coming and going. My career in London resurrected again after the war, and that was where our future was to be. We all came back to London in 1947, when we lived at 27 Bloomsbury Square. I did wonder whether we may have stayed and made our future in Frome, but our scope there would have been very limited, and I did have my career already set up in the City.

What were you doing with the RAF?

It was all signals, taking and passing on messages. I was in the follow up party that went to Normandy. This was in August 1944, France was liberated then and we quickly moved through and ended up in Brussels. My only other wartime trip abroad was when we were sent to India by boat. This trip was completed, but by the time we got there, the war in the east had ended.

In the late forties I remember Conigre House very well, and also in the wartime when we lived there, I went there right up until the time your mother died. It was after that when I went to Frome every Easter and summer holidays, on my own.

My mother's funeral was on Cup Final day in 1950, and Arsenal were playing Liverpool. My brother in law, John Matthews, and I slipped off occasionally from the gathering to listen to the match on the radio.

You didn't go and join the little crowd that would watch the match on the television in Woodmancy's shop window?

No, but talking about football, and I know that this is a bit later. But do you remember that I went to see Frome Town play Leyton Orient in the fifties, when they got to the 1st Round proper of the FA Cup. I travelled down with the Leyton Orient supporters on their special train. When they all got off at Frome Station, none of the 200 or so people knew where to go, so I had to direct them to the ground, via the town centre. There were no special buses or club officials there to meet them.

Yes, that match was on the 30th of November 1954, and you gave me the programme. I have lost it now, which is a pity, because it is a collector's item.

Any other snippets of information from the past that were handed down?

None from the Swaine side, but there was something from my mother's family which was told to me. It was that one of their ancestors was transported from one side of the Bristol Suspension Bridge to the other in a basket supported on a wire. This would have been before the construction was finished. His name would have been Shelton, but I don't know any more than that.

There was a twelve-year gap from the time that the towers were finished until the bridge was put in. I do believe that they strung a basket across to bring over materials. The basket could also hold a man and there is a rumour that Brunel himself actually had a ride in the basket. He did not though, live to see the bridge finished which was about the year 1864. But that is very interesting.

PART THREE

Origins of the Town and Frome's Woollen Heritage.

W Swaine set up his tailoring business at Catherine Hill in 1837. This was well before the railways came to Frome, and it was a time when the local woollen industry had dramatically declined. His confidence must have been high for a buoyant future, because in 1841 he expanded and moved *Onto The Bridge* at number 6.

Here, as we have seen before, the business was to stay until the 1930's when it was caught up in the depressed times, when the multiple shops were beginning to have an impact on the small trader. The three generations who had run the business kept the shop going and maintained it as the prime tailors to the town. They also had been military tailors for Frome when many hundreds of soldiers were billeted there during the First World War.

It is worth looking back and making a brief study of how and why Frome became so strong in the cloth industry, its rise and decline, and also why the town became the regional leader.

The origin of the town stems from the time that St Aldhelm arrived to build a church and a monastic settlement. Aldhelm, who was Abbott of a monastery at Malmsbury, was also a missionary and benefactor. He had set out to spread the gospel and offer a better life to the tribes and hermits who inhabited Selwood Forest.

The church which he built in Frome was on the site of the present church. and has been altered two or three times since, with the last rebuilding to its present form being in 1852. The first siting of the church, which is in an unusual position being halfway up a hill, must have something to do with the availability of fresh water from a spring, which runs right past the site. The water of this, can still be seen today running down the middle of Cheap Street. The following growth of the town, which is on one side of a river valley, gave it a character quite unlike any other. People who come here, whether they are visitors or residents, find it very easy to love the place.

It was in the period after the Anglicised Christians had left Rome for England in 596, that the town was founded. This was the time when the 'dark ages' were coming to an end. The geographic location proved to be ideal for the settlement to grow, firstly into a substantial village, and then become a parish and develop into a market town. Both the inaugurations of the parish and the market were before the Battle of Hastings.

The town survived the invasion of the Danish Vikings around 865, with the small population enjoying a certain freedom right through to 1066. The defeat of Harold by William of Normandy in 1066 was obviously a major turning point in English history, and is when the manorial control came into being. Whereby the inhabitants had enjoyed their previous free life, in an area controlled by the king, everything was about to change. The masses were to go into bondage under the new feudal system.

With the arrival of the Norman period, the invading King soon wished to know everything about the country he had conquered. To do this he had details of every area of the country documented in the Domesday Book. Frome is stated as having 109 heads of households, which indicates a population of about 500 people. There is reference to the market in the Domesday Book, implying that Frome was already a place of some importance. Life went slowly on through that mediaeval period, with Frome coming under the control of several manorial ownerships.

After the dissolution of the monasteries in 1539, the church lands passed into the hands of the Thynne family, who later bought more land in the area to build up the Longleat estate.

All this time the making of woollen cloth had quietly gone on, with nearly all of the production being done in or around the cottages. Wool had become more profitable than corn to produce, which led to more intensity and it was soon to become the country's most vital raw material.

Wool provided prosperity in various degrees to all who worked with it, from the sheep farmer right through to the clothier working at his cutting table. There were more sheep on this island than there were people.

Farmers, whether they be lords, clergy or smallholders sought to provide more and more sheep to feed the expanding industry. The momentum of the industry created wealth, and there was the other by-product, which shouldn't be forgotten - mutton.

The industry survived and grew through its primitive state, even to be undaunted by the Black Death of 1348. The plague wiped out more than a third of the population and set the Feudal System into disarray. The peasants who survived realised that they could then sell their labour to the highest bidder and not be tied to one master.

Later, through the Tudor and Stuart times, the woollen industry was expanding so fast that even more sheep needed to be reared. The enclosing of fields became the method to achieve this and production intensified. The West of England also received fleeces from Ireland, with regular shipments being brought in through the ports of Minehead and Bridgwater, (this route may also have brought in some migrant workers to the area). Packhorses carried the woolpacks to their destinations along the myriad of trails, which crossed the land. The finished woollen cloth was in great demand by the users in this country, with the producers toiling to keep up with demand. The governments of the day, saw the raw material as a great export earner. They channelled much of out of the country to bring in revenue, but it was not a popular move at home. The manufacturers soon got up in arms and the practice had to be curtailed. The merchants had enough difficulty in getting supplies for themselves, without seeing the precious raw material going to their competitors abroad.

Frome attracted an influx of workers from other parts of the country with the West of England prospering. The mixture of new people led to a diversity of religions in the town. With the Act of Uniformity in religion being imposed in 1662, much of the population followed the non-conformist church.

The period after this was one of great productivity, which led to Frome becoming the largest wool town in the region. Other towns with better communications gradually caught up and got ahead, but this was a little golden period for the place. Other towns had better road links with some having the added luxury of a navigable river. Frome's river was to turn a great many water-wheels, but it couldn't carry cargo boats.

All was not plain sailing, these were busy times for the artisans, but also times of discontent were on the horizon. The workers could see their efforts contributing greatly to the wealth of the town, but also see how the wealth was being distributed; not much in the way of life's comforts was coming their way.

Although the Frome artisans worked a six-day week, their lot in life was much better than those of the new northern factory mills. Life in Frome took some beating then, just as it does today.

The spinning of wool is a skill that goes back to the ancient Greeks, but that was in a very basic form with the operator teasing thread onto a simple bone or stick spindle. That simple form would have been an activity of the earliest Frome settlers. Humble dwellers would have had no option other than to seek a living from their natural surroundings.

The town grew up in a river valley at a point where it was convenient to ford the river, the hill on which it is built being a spur of the Mendips. The hills follow the river for some way and are integral to the Frome story. There were actually two clear water springs running down from the top of the hill above the town and these were of obvious significance, not only to the position of the original church, but also to in the early siting of houses. As we have seen, the settlement grew to become, at its peak, the largest wool town in the West of England.

The earliest clues to the importance of wool to the town are in the 1200's, when the wool trade was developing onwards from being just a cottage industry. This was the time when the spinning wheel had been reinvented from its origins in the Far East Extended families all worked in a different capacity to produce an end product, which was cloth. Mechanisation was still a long way off and would not appear until the mid 1700's.

Sheep would have been reared on the downlands that surrounded the town in Keyford, Marston, Whatley, Buckland Dinham and many other such places nearby. The owners supplying the women folk with the raw material to begin the spinning. Weavers (usually men of the family) would take the yarn after the spinning and make up cloth on their hand-operated looms. These often may be in their homes, or more likely in adjoining sheds or workshops nearby. The producing of cloth was a very intense affair with several spinners feeding one weaver. Teasels, the little prickly plants used to raise the nap in the cloth were available locally, and that was the next operation after the weaving.

The woollen cloth industry was the centre of Frome's trade, with the good central location making it a distribution centre for the locality. The Market Place, which was the town's focal point for trading, was an outlet for the family produced items, but bulk cloth though, would be sold to travelling representatives for transportation to the larger markets of the big cities.

Wool, then later cotton and silk were the raw materials used in production. Linen which comes from Flax plants would certainly have been spun, and also muslin. Linen, which also derives from ancient times, and was the popular product because of its comfort, as compared to wool. Woollen clothes and blankets would be an absolute necessity for the long cold winters, but the smoother cooler cloths were much appreciated in the summer.

In those early days, the wind of change was slow, one generation would pass on their skills to the next, with hardly an adjustment to their routines. Maybe a new blend of wools would become fashionable, or there were improvements to the spinning operation along the way. A loom might be improved or enlarged, but generally things would just go on just the same as they always had. People didn't expect any changes to their routines, and as it was to prove later, would strongly resist any changes that may be offered.

Women had spun wool merrily in their hovels for centuries, with their families helping out. These family units had grown into a very substantial industry, but what they didn't have was business sense on a larger scale. This passive workforce had become ripe for being taken over by powerful business-minded people who could control the markets and then the production. Entrepreneurs started to control most of the cloth distribution by the 15th and 16th centuries. They were skimming off large profit margins from this most buoyant of industries and becoming rich.

The merchants, who gained control of the domestic system, had taken almost complete control over the cottage producers. They would buy raw wool from farmers and take it around to the cottages. The cottagers then had to wash the wool, sort the long strands from the short, comb the fibres and then perform the spinning.

A view of what a typical peasant's cottage would have looked like before the Industrial Revolution.

The historic artisans houses at Sheppards Barton which survived the times of slum clearance. Now very much part of the Frome Heritage Trail.

Once this was done, the merchant collected the spun yarn, paid for it and left a new batch of raw wool. He then took the yarn to the weavers who wove it into cloth. Other treatments then had to be applied to the cloth such as fulling, which was a treatment to thicken and stretch the material. After that, there was the operation of combing the fibres of the cloth, and then there was the possibility that it had to be dyed. By this time it was generally taking about ten spinners to produce enough yarn for one weaver. It was an industry of ever increasing intensity.

One other plant, which grew abundantly in the district, was the woad. From this blue dye could be produced, which led to another branch of the textile industry developing. Frome became famous for its blue dye, and along the way many things got named after this, one being the Blue Coat Boys of the Blue House.

Dye works needed the facility of the river for their messy processes, as did the fullers, but it was still to be a good while before the water wheel was to appear to drive the spinning and weaving machines. There would have been one or two water wheels operating in the 15th and 16th centuries but these were for iron workings and corn grinding, with the largest corn mill owned by the Lord of the Manor.

The cloth industry in Frome was so strong by the mid.1600's, that the eye of the new industrialists had been caught who were not necessarily wool manufacturers. They could see more potential than was being realised at the time, and again things were about to change.

John Sheppard, and others came in, who soon invested in the building of new workshops. Anticipating the future benefit of waterpower some took sites beside the river. Sheppard, followed by his son, built firstly in Willow Vale and then at Spring Gardens. They also saw the benefit of providing sound housing for their workers and of course big houses for themselves. Sheppard's Barton being a prime example of cottages built for workers, and these still survive today. Although they were close to being pulled down in the drive for new development in the 1960's. The big houses that the owners built for themselves were well away from those of their employees, in a different part of the town.

So great was the output by the Frome cloth producing work-force, that in the late 1600's, provision was made to improve living conditions generally. An estate of terrace housing was begun, partly to suit the needs of the locals, but also to attract workers from other areas. Many had been persuaded to leave the 'Guild' towns where the working practices could be quite restrictive.

This piece of early housing development reinforced the town's belief in its continued wealth and also appeared to show confidence in the people who were producing it. The housing was of course the Trinity, and it pre-dated its northern equivalent by about 150 years. This housing now is appreciated for its historical significance, but again there was a big drive to have it pulled down, thankfully a good part of it has survived.

Most of the surrounding villages and hamlets also had become well involved in the wool industry. Following the pattern of the Frome families, but on a much smaller scale. The whole area was booming, and Frome was the leading cloth centre, without doubt. The population had grown so quickly that the town had at this time had more inhabitants than either Bath or Salisbury.

Wool would be coming into the town from much further afield now. This to feed the ever-growing demand. It came from places such as the Mendip Hills, Salisbury Plain and the Wiltshire Downs, all brought in by chains of packhorses.

Various ancillary trades had evolved to support the wool trade, and one of these was carding. This is the process of lifting and inter-weaving the fibres of the cloth to make it a much more attractive product. The cards comprised of fine metal wires fixed to the card, which were lightly moved over the woven cloth. Formerly this was done by hand using teasels, but demand had outstripped the supply of these plants. Carding came into its own as an industry within an industry.

Dozens of establishments set themselves up to provide carding and other associated services, but one of these firms grew to eventually take over the whole output for Frome. They were the firm, who later became S. Rawlings & Sons and stayed in existence for over 200 years, right through until 1972. Long before this time the demand for cards had subsided, but the firm had diversified, and produced many other commodities such as brushes and belt drives. being required to drive just about every machine in a mill or mechanised factory.

It was not until as late as 1720 that the first houses were built 'across the river' on the north side. Among the first of these was the small terrace next to the railway bridge in Willow Vale. Much growth soon took place on that side with the expansion of the woollen trade into its mechanised period. Nowadays of course, that side of the river is so developed that the Market Place is very central to the town. For so long, that was not the case.

A material, which was new to Europe had now been imported to Britain, and was causing quite a sensation on its arrival. It was cloth made from cotton, and had arrived from India.

The process of extracting cotton from the plant and weaving it into a fabric, had firstly developed in that country, but once it had been seen in Europe, around the 1600's, the demand became insatiable.

This material was much lighter than the wool or linen based fabrics, it could also be woven with lively patterns. The demand meant that many clever brains were working overtime to think of ways to speed up the cloth producing process. All classes of people wanted cotton, they liked the light material next to their skin, and also the gaiety of colours that were coming along. The further expansion of the industry was hotting up.

Significant industrial developments were being made elsewhere in the country from the early 1700's, which would have far reaching effects on Britain's future. They would directly lead this country being the world's leaders in industry and generate an 'Industrial Revolution.'

In Staffordshire, Abraham Darby pioneered the use of coke as a fuel to be used to smelt iron in a furnace. This was to lead to the mass-producing of cast iron made in moulds and provide the ability for large castings to be made. It also co-incided with the development of steam power, which was to ensure that a very different future was about to emerge. Formerly charcoal was the fuel used to heat iron ore, but this provided much less heat than coke.

The new methods and associated inventions had a profound effect on people and the places where they lived. Mass production in factories was providing goods to the general public that had previously only been available to the upper classes. A new middle class of managers had sprung up and so had demand. The population was increasing rapidly in the producing areas, which was bringing new social problems. But the new methods had produced an unstoppable charge into ever increasing production. All this had the effect of bringing down prices and expanding the general economy.

The need of the basic worker was very apparent, with the most prudent industrialist providing sound housing for his people. And this would be close to the place of work. Frome had already provided terraces of artisan's houses, with the northern towns and cities now following suit. Expansion was on a massive scale nationwide, with Manchester taking the lead for the cloth industry.

Cotton fabrics were by now the product which dominated the cloth industry and soon many other countries were taking up cotton growing. Including America, whose plantations spread like wildfire right across the southern states from Memphis to Charleston.

The one great invention, which did lead to the speeding up of cloth production, was the invention of the Spinning Jenny. This was by James Hargreaves in 1764, and in one stroke the old spinning wheel was made redundant. Whereas the spinning wheel could spin raw wool, cotton, or linen into yarn on a single wheel, the Spinning Jenny could spin multiple reels at one time.

Hargreaves invention was manually operated, but very soon afterwards a northern wigmaker called James Arkwright was to bring in another innovation. He developed a water frame, which mechanised and enlarged the Spinning Jenny, this was powered by a water-wheel. He patented the device, and made himself very rich by licensing the product out to anyone who wanted to use it. He was astute enough though, to make a condition that any mill wishing to use it must have at least 100 Jennies operating. At a stroke this began factory style production, and sent the industry into freefall.

Arkwright's invention ushered in the era of mass production with all that this entailed - consumerism, booms, slumps and unemployment.

From the 1770's Frome's cloth industry became mechanised, with the introduction of mills which could spin and weave. The days of the family production of cloth in their homes was effectively over. Within the next fifty years some 200 water wheels would appear along the River Frome and its tributaries. The Industrial Revolution had caught up with the town in a big way.

It was not all to be plain sailing and harmony for the new work methods. The artisans who had produced in the same way for centuries were justifiably afraid that the new machines would be putting them out of work. There were riots on the streets of Frome when new mills were being built. The new methods left the people extremely worried about their future. Mill owners had to be very alert and secretive at this time, sometimes setting up a new mill well away from the local hostility. In reality jobs were not a problem, especially for women, because so many of the new jobs just consisted mundane work such as machine minding. Men who had been weavers did not fare so well and were driven out of work, most of those had to seek new occupations. Some would migrate to other regions or even take their families abroad.

There became such a desperate shortage of people to perform the menial tasks, that children from the age of eight were used in great numbers. The owners didn't mind this as children didn't have to be paid as much as adults. It was to be a very long time before any consideration was given to the rights of employees.

The bulk of workers by this time had built up resentment against their rich employers. They could see their efforts providing huge profits for the rich bosses, whilst their families had the scraps and lived on the breadline.

1800's.

The intense workings of the mills around Frome was to be relatively short lived. Cotton cloth was the material in most demand and the northern mills had been very quick to modernise. They brought in steam engines to replace water wheels and the factory-mills became relentless. They drove hundreds and hundreds of Jennies, all feeding the demand for more cloth. Equally the demand for the raw material was ever more intense, with the factories needing the supplies to be reliably delivered to their doors.

Canals had been built to move the large bales of cotton from the ports to the factories, and to supply coal to feed the steam engines. This new method of transport dramatically cut down the delivery time and cut costs. Roads and road transport were also slow with only limited reliability. The canal network soon spread right across the country and was intensely used right through the 1800's. Frome almost had a canal when the construction for one had started near to Welsh Mill. The intention was to link with the coalmines around Radstock, but the scheme lost its way and was not to be.

With the Industrial Revolution now in full flow, much interest was being shown in the new invention, that of a steam engine running on rails. Static steam engines had been built a hundred years before and had been successfully used in the removing of water from mines. But a man named Trevithick from Cornwall had shown the way in 1804, when his locomotive pulled a 10-ton load on rails for a distance of 10 miles.

Soon competitions were being set to find the most efficient design of a steam engine. Trevithick's locomotive had proved unreliable and the final winner at the 1829 Rainhill Trials was George Stephenson's 'Rocket.'

The Liverpool to Manchester Railway was to open in 1830, with a train headed by 'Rocket,' and despite a few setbacks, this mode of transport was set to be the dominant British transport system of the 19th century.

Manchester, soon to be followed by Notts and Yorkshire, all led the way with cloth manufacture, and because of this Frome was to pay the price. Steam engines had been introduced in the north, to replace water-wheels, therefore they had lost the dependency on the variables of waterpower. Steam powered mills could, and did, operate 24 hours a day.

By the 1820's Frome was in depressed times, they had not the will or ability to keep up with their northern counterparts. Foreign suppliers naturally sent their ships to the northern ports, where the best prices were paid.

The River Frome quickly became an industrial wasteland and the remaining mills, of those still working, were reduced to just a few. There was only one clothier who had introduced steam power to a mill - he was John Sheppard at Spring Garden. This was introduced in 1811 and it was to stay with them until 1878 when, even they had to call it a day.

All the terraces of workers houses, which had so encouragingly been built a couple of centuries earlier, began to fall in to disrepair, many becoming empty. For the following hundred years they would now be thought of as a liability to the town. Only one mill remained in operation in Frome through to the middle of the twentieth century, that was Tuckers at Wallbridge. They had modernised to suit the times as best they could, but in 1965 they too finally wound up.

In the late Middle-Ages silk weaving developed in Britain. The first silk mill to benefit from a waterwheel was at Derby where a five-storey throwing mill was built. Throwing being the process, which prepares silk thread for weaving.

By the end of the 1700's silk mills became very popular with free-trade policies leading to a glut of production. With the material being highly sought after, it's not surprising that many English silk mills got founded, and one of these was at Frome.

The Frome silk mill was in the heart of the town between Merchants Barton and the river, quite close to where the first monastic settlement was built. The mill, founded in 1845, operated through until the 1920's, when production ceased. In the same way that cloth mills had succumbed to steam power, so did the silk mills. Another of the products which the Frome Silk Mill produced was crepe. Whereby in centuries past, silk had been a secret process, the manufacture of crepe still was. Anybody working in that part of the factory was under oath not to reveal any of the working processes.

The industrial history of Frome has not been well documented over the centuries. Had it been a Guild town, that might have been different, but it was not to be. So much has been lost both in the physical and written form, that much of the general history has to be pieced together. If we believe the written statement that there were 200 wheels on the river, it takes some imagination as to what they comprised. It may well be that the number is exaggerated, but it does tell us of the intensity of the period and the chase into mechanisation, with the pursuance of dreams of new wealth and purpose.

Water Power

A water wheel is a simple and obvious invention. Man has always needed tools to maintain the ability to live and survive, and the water wheel when attached to a spindle does provide a very powerful turning device. When a smaller wheel edged with cogs is fitted at the other end of the spindle, there is an incredibly useful source of power being offered. The vertical wheel was developed in Britain from the 13th century, horizontal and vertical wheels had been used abroad as far back as Biblical times.

The grinding of corn into flour was always a laborious and slow task when done by hand. This was an obvious candidate for the water-wheel once it had been developed into an efficient machine. Another early use for a mill was in iron workings where the power source could be directed to power a very large pounding hammer. After the configuration of a mill and the operations for corn grinding had been worked out, the other important question to be considered was in the siting of a mill.

To put a large water wheel anywhere on a river is an option and water will turn it. But the wheel's efficiency is only as good as the force of the river current, and this can be quite variable. The flow of water against the wheel needs to be controllable as far as possible and that includes stopping the source altogether, although a simple wheel can be braked.

It was very soon realised that the best siting, was at a point on a river where there is a natural weir. The wheel can then be located to the side of the weir and be fed by a sluiceway. The water can pass a sluice gate and fall to drive the water wheel in a controlled manner before discharging back into the river beyond the weir. The forming of a side channel in itself is enough to provide a forceful flow of water.

How then does this affect the woollen mills that are suddenly springing up in the 1770's? They were too late to get the prime sites, for these were taken by the flourmills who had arrived two or three hundred years before. Even those best sites were susceptible to the variations of the river flow. After a good bout of rainfall any wheel could be turned, but there were times of drought and low rainfall which affected the water movement on a non-tidal river.

These new mill owners had to choose positions as best they could, and use any trick they could think of to get their wheels turning. Mostly they had to look for any point where the river flowed just a little bit faster and make the best of it. But there was one other solution to operate a water-wheel, which was to prove more efficient and reliable.

The problem of improving water-wheel efficiency was not just for Frome, but a problem to be solved nationwide. Water-power was in its heyday, and as we have seen at Frome, mills were required in great numbers. It was soon to be realised that there was another method of supplying water to a water-wheel. This is where water could be dropped from above onto a wheel, and is known as 'overshooting.' If upturned troughs are fitted to the ends of each fin of a water-wheel, and a trickle of water supplied from above. The water would fill every trough on one side of the wheel and turn it. With the water supply being constant the wheel must keep turning. How fast the wheel may turn would depend on the amount of water being supplied or by the size of the wheel. Again, this was not a new invention but one regenerated from the past to suit the new times.

In the 1750's a British engineer made a test to see which type of water-wheel was the more efficient, the undershot type or the overshot. The published results revealed that the overshot type had about twice the efficiency as the undershot.

There is one thing that is in abundance in the Mendips and its adjoining hills, which now could come into play. A source which was instrumental in the development of Frome in the first place, and that is spring-water.

Together with hill streams and brooks there was a ready supply of water falling from a higher level. There must have been enough water because, as we have said before, a canal was planned and started above the river near Welsh Mill, and canals require plenty of water to keep them replenished.

Many a spring or hill stream would have been diverted into a culvert and directed towards a mill with an overshot wheel. Leats may be cut to divert streams from an adjoining valley, all directed to the Frome and Mells rivers. It is easy to make a holding reservoir or artificial pond in a suitable location above a mill. Holding reservoirs would provide water for a surge to start the wheel turning, or give a bit more power as necessary. The lake in Orchardleigh Park is artificial, having been formed by making a dam; below this at Old Ford there were some very efficient mills

The Mells River has a good number of tributaries running down from the hills into it. These all end up boosting the flow of the River Frome where they merge just beyond Spring Gardens. What that area must have been like in the heyday of the water wheel really does extend the imagination.

Roads and Transport

Back in the Middle Ages there were no established roads, and not even many wagon-ways. All transportation to do with the wool trade was done by packhorses, with the woolpack being the recognised load.

Packhorse trails criss-crossed the countryside, in what may seem like a haphazard fashion. But the trails were taking the shortest possible route between any two places. They may go around a field to avoid a landowner's property, but they appeared where the minders wanted to go, and they were very numerous.

Other people obviously used them as well, and if any particular group, such as the clergy, had a vested interested in a particular route, they would take care of it. Maintenance was particularly needed for a hollow-way through a wood.

These days, some of these trails may have developed into roads, some into bridal paths, and others into footpaths. Others will have disappeared altogether with the progress of things.

Through the seventeenth and eighteenth centuries wheeled traffic was severely disadvantaged. Not just because of atrocious roads, but because of government legislation that was in hand at the time. Rather than have a road-upgrading plan, they put limitations the use of wheeled traffic. The thinking being that all these wheels damaged the tracks, and were a hazard to foot and packhorse traffic. Roads were nothing more than mud tracks with stone or gravel randomly thrown down. Most were rutted so badly that travel was painfully slow, in winter many became impassable. A wagon from Frome to London took two and a half days to complete the journey.

The cloth trade had become the country's leading industry and a better system of roads was urgently needed for trade generally. Without the facility of getting goods quickly and safely to the main London markets, trade and exports were being compromised. The government had to do something about it, and in 1763 the first Turnpike Act was authorised. The Turnpike Trust was set up to control, improve, and maintain roads all across the country.

The only problem for the traveller was that they were all to be charged tolls to use them, and not surprisingly this caused much indignation. Toll bars with the little cottages beside them sprung up all along these Turnpike roads, and many of these cottages still stand today.

The Turnpike Trust was responsible for the upkeep of the open roads, but not through the towns. Inside a parish boundary the responsibility was solely that of the parish, and there was usually a marking sign or stone to show the boundary.

The quality of the early Turnpikes was very patchy, but the system was good enough for mail-coach services to start in 1774. Stage-coach services also got under way also and the time taken for travellers to complete journeys was drastically reduced.

This also became the golden age for coaching inns, with a big industry building up to manage the travellers and the horses. When the railways arrived some sixty years later, travelling habits were to again change dramatically. The golden age of the coaching inn was to have a relatively short life.

Much study was done to ascertain what might be the best surface for the new Turnpike roads. The answer was provided by a man called Macadam, whose method comprised the compacting of layers of stones. The stones would be of all about the same size. They would have sharp edges so that they would bind together when mixed with mud. Not rounded stones, which would have a tendency to roll against each other and be unstable. (It was many years later when tar was added to the stones, to be called Tar-Macadam).

All the main routes out of Frome had Turnpikes - to Radstock, Bath, Warminster and Shepton Mallet. The little sign in Bridge Street shows the Parish boundary, beyond which the Turnpike started, and not far away would be the toll-bar and Pikemans cottage. Bridge Street was the northerly route out of town before North Parade and Fromefield were built in 1797. Before this the road from Bridge Street swung out towards Welsh Mill.

The new road system did dramatically improve travel times, and a Flying coach (Flying meaning non-stop except for horse changes), left the Crown Hotel at 6pm, had an arrival time at its destination in London of noon the next day. The first stop for a change of horses was Norton St Philip.

Mail-coaches and Stage-coaches were able to set up regular schedules, with the Mail-coaches being exempt from toll charges. The mail guard blew his long horn as they approached a tollgate and expected the gates to be open ready for them to pass through. The Mail-coaches were so regular and punctual that towns and villages used their arrical to check their clocks by. Milestones were placed beside the roads and the mail guard could check their progress against his timepiece.

Turnpike roads had everything their own way until the coming of the railways. Then the Pikemans cottages soon became redundant, right up until today no further use was found for them.

After the tolls were removed, the roads were not to come into their own again until the motorcar was to make an appearance about 50 years later, during this time, they again tended to fall into disrepair.

An old print of The Bridge looking towards the west side. St John's Church is in the distance with The Blue House in the foreground. The Bluecoat boys are at play on the bridge.

The Market Place

Frome always was a working town, and a critical part of that was the market. A market being the most efficient way for trading, thereby enriching the lives of the people. The market adds to the town's prosperity and also attracts people from the outlying villages, thereby giving interaction between the locals. It becomes the focal point of the area.

The market was probably first set up outside the church gates, which was the general tradition. With natural growth it would have needed to move to a more spacious location, and this is where the road widens at the lower and flatter part of the town. A cross is a market symbol, which remains from the original links with the church. A deal struck below the cross with a clap of the hands, was as binding as a written contract of today.

A town was not just able to create a market and call itself a Market Town, it had to obtain a Royal Charter direct from the local King. A charter was not automatically given, the town had to fit in with the Saxon structure of the area. It also had to be of a certain stature and also in a location that was pivotal to the surrounding villages. There also a stipulation of a certain distance from the next Market Town. It could also, only operate on two designated days of a week. There was also scope for a one-off special market or fair once a year. People would use these to stock up for the winter, when many of the roads became impassable

With the market having moved locations somewhere in the late Anglo-Saxon period, traders would then have to pay rent to the King. Later after the Norman Conquest when the market came under the auspices of the Lord of the Manor, he would collect the rents.

The system of operation which was to define the traditional English market, amazingly set up a pattern of trading which was to progress right through the centuries and up to the present day. In the last couple of hundred years though, the organisation of the markets has passed into the hands of the local councils.

Trinity Housing

Frome was made prosperous when it grew into a wool-manufacturing centre. Firstly as a conglomeration of cottage industries and then later when mechanised. With the running down of the cloth industry from the middle of the 19th century, these cottages began to fall into disrepair and a slow decline in their upkeep had begun, many became empty.

By the 1920's and 1930's they had become slums, which lacked basic amenities such as electric light and proper toilets. More started to be abandoned and generally there was no attention paid to them.

It was not until the 1950's when Britain was starting to come out of the post war austerity years, that they became a prime target for removal.

So long had they been ignored and considered a liability, that no thought was given to their history. It was a general trait nationwide for little interest to be shown in industrial history. Frome Town Council had placed a slum clearance order on the properties, and rightly wanted to provide as much new housing as possible for the community.

The country was experiencing better times again, with young home seekers demanding all the new innovations and facilities that modern housing could provide. Still more than one in ten homes did not have a bathroom.

The Macmillan government of the time was boldly stating that 'You've never had it so good' and boasted of the three hundred thousand new homes which had been built in the last year. They wanted the trend to continue and gave local councils the backing to proceed.

The demolition started in the Trinity area and new homes were built, although their design left something to be desired. Council housing of that period followed the same sort of banal designs right across the country. Everything seemed set for this trend to continue.

One thing that was getting overlooked amongst all this enthusiasm for demolition was the historic value of some of these buildings.

There was almost panic amongst the authorities in their quest to follow the government leads. It was something they could do, and did do, they fed a new boom in housing.

There was certainly no thought given in any way to upgrading what was there already, that certainly was not on the agenda, conservation was not a word that was on anybody's lips.

It was only when a few local people stood up and started to make some noises that any notice began to be taken. At least they slowed down the destruction and made other people aware of what was happening to this historic part of old England.

A build up in numbers of protesters developed into a pressure group. They got momentum going and pointed out in no uncertain terms to the Frome Town Council, the historic significance of the Trinity area. The campaign began to get much publicity, and in 1972 even the influential 'Architects Journal' had run a feature. It was only after this, that the tide began to turn, but it was to be a couple of years yet until the council was convinced.

The delay that these people caused was just enough to save some of the terraces. At the turn of the 1970's, the country as a whole was reacting to the mass demolition of big areas in historical towns and cities. A trend towards conservation had not yet begun, but the general public could see for themselves that the design quality of the replacement buildings held much to be desired. In most cases the new buildings were totally out of scale with the surroundings, and the designs had little sympathy to any local history.

One author, Colin Amery, published a book in 1975 called 'The Rape of Britain,' in which he detailed the appalling destruction, which was underway in thirty British towns. Frome was one of those towns featured.

It was not only housing developments, which were threatening Frome, but also roads. There were radical plans to run a new road right across the town centre, from Badcox through Willow Vale. Fortunately though, plans for a new by-pass went ahead and this curtailed any interest in road development within the town.

Now that the cattle marked has moved from its old town-centre site, there is no great pressure of road traffic using the town. Gone are the days when a thousand vehicles an hour crossed The Bridge.

PART FOUR

Family History 1836 - 1962

We will have been particularly fortunate, if we have been left some good family documentation and photographs by our departed loved ones. Many will have left us before we gleaned an intimate knowledge of their early life. We must cherish any snippets of information that had been given to us in the past about how they lived. Our recorded past is available for us to discover, but detailed information is not. How often do we look at an old photograph and wish that somebody had written on the back the names of the people in the picture.

Clues to the past must be unearthed to find our Family Heritage. Collected and pieced together they will make up the story. Genetic history is becoming increasingly important to our dependants, and the recording of facts essential. Any remote statement or fragment of information will assist in the formation of the bigger picture. A search into the depths of memory may get a recall of an interesting statement that a relative had once said.

The available family tree is the starting point, compiling as much detail as possible about our Great Grandfathers, and before. Not forgetting, firstly, to interrogate all those elder friends and relatives who are still living, about their lives and memories. To get information before 1840, the main source of facts would come from Church records, because detailed records only begun on that date.

My Research

It was in the early 1990's that I found that I had some additional time on my hands. This was due to a redundancy, and an eye-opening experience it was too. Having been working continuously since 1959, it was a shock to the ego to be suddenly put out of work, and being put into the position of having to find work at a time when just about every practice in my profession was shedding staff.

This was the architectural profession, and over the following four years I did find oddments of work. But I had found myself mixed up in what was to be the biggest building slump since the war.

The staffing numbers in the profession were to be reduced by some two-thirds at this time.

Since then I have got back into what had become a leaner and computerised profession, but I did make good use of the barren spells that were enforced on me, in fact the experience was to change my whole outlook on life.

I had decided to use the enforced mid-life break to do some things that I otherwise might not have been able to do until retirement, and perhaps not even then. Among the things that I studied and pursued were photography, computers, and family history.

During one summer when I didn't have much to do, I decided to travel around the country to visit some of the preserved steam railways that had sprung up. This was a chance to make use of some of my new-found photographic skills and to experience some nostalgia as well.

The photography went so well that a publisher became interested in the set of pictures, and I had a book published.

My childhood interest in steam trains had all but completely diminished during the 20 years that I was bringing up a family. It was nice to make an adult study of the subject and learn many things that I had never known as a boy, this I could then reflect in the book.

My interest in family history also grew, and I was able, on many occasions, to join up with my father and make trips back to our old hometown of Frome. A few of his old friends and contacts were still alive, and they provided some interesting material. It was an opportunity that would not have been there a few years later. After this my family research and interest in the Frome history had grown to such an extent that we were able to extend it into the making of this book.

During the early research I was able to obtain from a company called Halberts in America, listings of every registered Swaine household world-wide. This was quite an eye-opener, and I decided to write to some of them. In fact I wrote to over 200. This included all 70 addresses in Australia, 10 in New Zealand, and also others in America and Canada, with extensive inquiries at home and in Ireland. I believe that these facilities of checking registered names are now available on the Internet.

With the biggest cluster of Swaines being in West Yorkshire, and with very many of these having histories in the woollen trade. I was keenly interested to see if I could find out if any had moved from Somerset. Especially during the times of the slump of the early 1800's, when the northern mills had modernised and left the West of England floundering. As such yet, there is not a definite lead, but this is my main aim of ongoing research and something may yet turn up.

With my communications to various families, it soon became apparent that I should always address my letters to Mr and Mrs of the household and not just the man. It is surprising just how many of the ladies are interested in the subject. And as it turned out, I realised that in my family, it was only the ladies of the family who had kept anything at all over the past 100 years.

My letters to the far-off places produced some excellent stories, and I have included extracts from these later in this section.

The Swaine Family of Frome were mainly Non-Conformists, and the records of the Non-Conformist Churches are not generally as well kept as those of other churches. However we do have sketchy family tree going back to John of the seventeenth century, which was a good start and linked the family to Christian Swayne of Bruton. That immediately showed that there would be variations in name spelling. The contents of that tree will always be under scrutiny and will need further verification and updating in due course. The family tree since 1840 is much fuller because reference can be made to the document Kelly's Directory, copies of which are kept at the Frome Library.

For how long have the Swaine family been in Frome, and what was their activity was before the tailoring business began in 1837. There is still so much to discover.

Early photographs of family members are very precious, and it essential that they are all identified. These days photography is commonplace, but a hundred or more years ago the ancestors may have only had one photograph taken in their lifetime.

As far as the name Swaine goes, it is very likely that someone along the line added the 'e.' One known origin of Swain comes from the Irish - Young Man, which derives from the invasion of Ireland by

King Sven of Denmark in the late 10th Century. Likeliest origins of the Somerset people are the definition names given to people, Swain - Country Youth or Young Lover.

In early days, many would have been illiterate, and the name would be recorded as it sounded, - perhaps Swayne. The Naval terms Coxswain and Boatswain are also likely to be relevant.

In some ways we are fortunate that the name Swaine is not too common, and other families of the same name could be contacted. The biggest concentration of Swaines in Britain is in West Yorkshire, - 228 registered households according to the computer register. In Somerset there are 8 households, none now in Frome. Many Swaines from different lines emigrated to the new worlds, and are scattered far and wide.

The author on his Lambretta with grandfather posing for the picture on the back. This photograph was taken about halfway down Willow Vale.

The spring water running down the centre of Cheap Street has always been an attraction for children, and nearly all put a foot in it as part of the growing up process.

Modern day view of Catherine Hill. A very hazardous route for wheeled traffic, but these days it is mostly reserved for the pedestrian. The small ornate lamp standard, made by the Cockey Company, is one to have survived the years.

The Search begins

To
Frome Public Library.
For the attention of The Librarian.
Justice Lane, Frome. BA11 1BE.25th,Feb 1993

Dear Sir/Madam. I am trying to trace my family ancestry. The family were tailors in the town from 1837-1936, and there are now no Swaines left in Frome. Please could you tell me if any of the church records are kept at the library? Also, if there might be anyone who could do a search for me.
Yours sincerely.

From
Deborah Hulbert, Reference Librarian, Frome Library. 26-2-1993

Dear Mr Swaine, Thank you for your enquiry. There is no central repository of parish records of Frome, but a local lady, Mrs Massey, does hold some of the parish records and may be willing to undertake a search for you. She also holds the local Censuses. I suggest you contact her (address enclosed). The Somerset Record Office in Taunton is the main repository of local records in Somerset, and is the best place to visit to conduct research. I enclose a leaflet about it - an appointment is necessary as the facilities are very well used.
Frome Library holds the local directories for the town and the Somerset Directory extracts for Frome. If you wish, I could go through them and photocopy any entries for Swaine. There would be a charge of ten pence per copy plus twenty-five pence P&P.
Yours sincerely.

To
Deborah Hulbert, The Library, Frome.

Thank you for your letter of the 26th Feb. and for all the information you have given. I would like copies of the extracts from the Frome

Directories, regarding Swaine entries. Please could you invoice me as you suggested. I have also written to Mrs Massey.
Yours sincerely.

To
Mrs H Massey, 8a, Critchill Grove, Frome.

Dear Mrs Massey, I hope you don't mind me writing to you, but I got your name from Deborah Hulbert of Frome Library, who said that you hold some of the parish records.
I am trying to trace my ancestors, the Swaine family, tailors on The Bridge until 1936. I do have a family tree going back to the 1700's, but it doesn't give much detail.
If you could undertake a search of the records, I would be very grateful. Before Christmas I visited Frome, and went to the Vallis Way cemetery, where there is a family grave. Enclosed is a transcript of the headstone. There should be an adjoining grave where James Treasure and Helen Frances Swaine (Neale) are buried, but I could see no stone, James Frederick was a member of the Volunteer Fire Brigade in the early part of this century.
Yours sincerely.

From
Mrs Hilda Massey, Critchill Grove, Frome.

3rd May. 1993
Dear Mr Swaine,
Thank you for your letter dated 1st March. 1 shall be happy to check Frome records for details of your family history. I usually ask for a small donation before I start, with the suggestion that a later donation can be added if I find a satisfactory amount of information. After deducting my postal costs, I share the donations between the Frome Museum and the Frome churches, roughly in proportion to the amount of work on each set of records.
Your Family appears to have been members of the Badcox Lane Baptist Church, which has been closed for many years. I already have a few notes about the Swaine Family, as I have had several

requests since 1960 for information about the Treasure family, and William Swaine married Elizabeth Treasure on 21st April 1834 at St Johns Church, Frome. James Treasure was a witness. They were both described as "of this parish", but from the census records I see that William was born in Bruton. Have you checked any censuses? If not I can look up the 1841,1851,1871, & 1881 for The Bridge, Frome.

There are earlier entries in our register for Swaine marriages, but as William was born in Bruton, I have no record of names of his parents. Do you want details of Elizabeth's parents or brothers and sisters? Several years ago a friend copied for me all the inscriptions in the Nonconformist cemetery in Vallis Way. She had "William Francis died June 4, 1849 aged 13". This agrees with the census. She also had "William Swaine who died Dec.13, 1889", but she may have made a mistake. She has "Also of Sarah Bessie Swaine". That is more helpful is that she copied the inscription on the second grave. Here it is: - "In loving memory of James Treasure Swaine, born Nov.2 1840, died Nov.8 1915, and Helen Francis Neale a Dec.1871-Sept.18 1961. Also of Jane Swaine died July 7,1941 aged 97 years"

I have a list of members of Badcox Lane Baptist Church in 1843 with the date of joining. James Treasure was a deacon in the church in that year. William Swaine, Bridge, joined in 1832. Ann Swain of Keyford joined in 1807.

I have just looked in the early burial records for nonconformist burials in Catherine Hill burial ground, a William Francis Swaine of The Bridge, was buried June 7, 1849 aged 12, son of William Swaine. James Treasure Swaine son of William Swaine, tailor, Catherine Hill, was buried 25 Aug. 1840 aged 19 months.

1 won't stop to check any more records, as I have a sale of Tradecraft goods in church on Friday and Saturday.

Perhaps you would let me know if, despite the birth of your William in Bruton, you still want earlier marriages from St Johns? I see from the index that there are about ten Swain marriages between 1763 & 1834, and a couple of baptisms, in 1789 & 1803.

I hope you are able to read my arthritic writing? I'm afraid I do not type.

Yours sincerely.

Searches to the Southern Hemisphere

54 Beaudesert Road,
Moorooka, Brisbane,
Queensland.
1992

Dear Geoffrey,

Thank you for your letter of interest, in concern with the surname of Swaine. Your letter interested me in wondering how someone some 12,000 miles away managed to locate me. Never the less am replying as someone with the same interest in Family History, having gone back in line on my fathers side to 1728.

Our family origins are in Hastings, East Sussex, with my grandfather Frederick Joseph John, born 7-11-1877. He married Annie Maria Crouch on 16-12-1900, died on 30 Aug.1936. One of four children whose brother Philip took passage to Canada.

I myself was born in Bridgwater, Somerset, but that being due to evacuation from Hastings during 1941.

Whether this information is of any use to you, or the current information of many years research that I've done may or may not tie in with your own, remains to be seen.

My earliest records go back to Joseph Swaine, born in Hastings on 5th June 1728, one of 6 children.

As a matter of interest, a very good recourse for genealogy research is the Church of Jesus Christ Latter Day Saints, who have the whole records for the United Kingdom available for those interested in family history.

Trust this may assist you in your search for family.

Yours sincerely,
John F. Swaine

27 Haig Street
Netherby.
S. Australia..
7 December 1992

Dear Mr. Swaine,

Your letter was delivered to our address on the 20th November. It was quite unexpected and also a pleasant surprise to think that somebody across the other side of the world had sat down and taken time to unravel what could prove to be an interesting story of migration and personal relationships.

For what ever reason the Swaine family have entrusted me with details of our short history in SA. I am only too happy to provide you with a concise statement, which may start to answer some of the questions that are in your mind. Families grow apart and consequently live separate lives. It is possible you will receive a response from other arms of the family who have received your letter. I hope we colonials don't appear to be affected by the noontime sun when you bring your mosaic together.

The SA Swaines arrived in about the late 1890's. They originated from Bradford. I have a seemingly ancient photograph of somebody alleged to be my grandfather working as a mill hand in a hamlet named Lobethal near Adelaide. It appears the skills were sought out by the mill owners and they agreed to migrate under a government scheme.

From this family sprung six children whose names are recorded on the enclosed sheet. You will see that I am included in the red family tree. There are living males carrying the Swaine name from the marriages of Joe and Dolly. However, divine presence has intervened and daughters have sprung from the matrimonial beds.

I have two sons, 17 & 15 years of age and my cousin David has two male anklebiters.

I am not aware of any discussion within the family of a connection with the Frome area of Somerset. This comes as a surprise to me.

For your information there is a family of Swaines living in Sydney. We as a group have never had any contact with them.

What I find very remarkable is the coincidence of names arising out of your correspondence. Stanley appears twice within the family and your address is Stanley Road. I am going to buy a ticket in the pools.

Yours sincerely, Gerald Swaine.

P.O. Box 24,
Yorkeys Knob 4871,
Queensland,
Australia.

My grandfather migrated to Australia from Yorkshire in 1912. He brought with him his wife, five daughters and three sons. All were employed in the woollen industry, and were brought to Australia by the Onkaparings Woollen Company which had a mill in a small town called Lobethal in the Adelaide Hills.

Grandad left England two weeks after the sinking of the Titanic, and sailed to Australia in a ship called the 'Jervis Bay'. During the First World War, the 'Jervis Bay' was converted into an auxiliary cruiser, and was sunk in action.

There is a man near here whose name is Swyny. He told me that he had visited the place from which his forebears had come - a small town in County Cork in Ireland, and examined all the records he could get his hands on. Then he said to me, 'I'll tell you something else - that is where your name comes from, it is all in the records of the births there'. The Swynys, Sweeneys and the Swaines came from that village according to Mr Swyny, who is an optometrist.

My brother has visited Bradford and met some of our relatives there. I don't know how you found my name and address, but it was fascinating to hear from you.

Yours sincerely,
Dr. Cyril D. Swaine.

33 Sullivan Crescent,
Wanniassa ACT 2903,
Australia.

19-11-92
My branch of the family lived in Ireland for several generations. I can recall being told by my father that the first Irish 'Swaine' was believed to have been a member of Cromwell's army of occupation,

and may of come from the west of England. From memory his name was Francis. The story goes that he was murdered by locals.

I understand that our family converted to Catholicism at some stage. This possibly took place at the height of the Irish nationalist/home rule movement last century.

Yours sincerely,
John Swaine.

Vale Farm,
Kingsbury Lane,
Waurn Ponds,
Victoria. 3221.

Our branch of the Swaine family came to Australia leaving Liverpool in 1862. They arrived in Melbourne in 1863, and were from Evercreech, Shepton Mallet.

They settled near Ballarat, Victoria.

Enos Swaine was only here 7 years when he was killed, and his widow married again a short time afterwards. My father was Stanley Victor (d.1984) 72yrs, grandson of the first settlers. Here follows part of the tree.

Enos, b. Stoney Stratton 1838, d. 1871, Aust. Married at Evercreech 1859 to Ann Southway (1839-1924). Children - James b.1861, John and Mary died in infancy. Enos John b.1870/d.1918. Married in 1898 to Edith Whittington and had 3 daughters and 4 sons, my father being the youngest. Two sons were drowned in 1925, and my father's brother died in 1991. I am one of 3 daughters and so the Swaine line stops with us. Apparently there were other members of the family who came about the same time, and settled on the south coast of Victoria. I have been unable to locate any descendants so far.

It is my dream to go to Evercreech and see the area from whence they came. Maybe next year my husband (Kevin), and I will have the opportunity to visit. Our children - Richard d.2yrs, Christine 28, Jennifer 26, John 22.

Yours sincerely, Margaret Lyons (Swaine)

Box 6309
Tweeed heads South,
New South Wales,
Australia.

Unfortunately my father Stanley Swaine, (now dec). was not one for talking of the past. He was the second of two sons (Edward is the eldest, whereabouts unknown, age 80 plus?), only two children came from the union of George and Ruth (nee Waddington) Swaine.

They came to Australia sailing from Morecambe in 1927 when my father was 10 years old. The family resided prior to that in Cliff Terrace, Station Road, Denholm, Nr. Bradford, and Lily Bank Cross -----? Heysham Road, Morecambe.

Great Grandfather Swaine lived in Field House, Denholm. The house still stands but is sub-divided.

On a trip to Albany, Western Australia recently, we came across an E. Swaine on the 1914-18 Honour Roll, which we intend to follow up.

Yours sincerely,
Richard and Barbara Swaine.

British Connection

47 Springdale Cres.
Bradford, Yorkshire

2-12-1992
Dear Mr Swaine,
My brother Peter received a letter from you showing an interest in the Bradford SWAINE name. Since I have done some training of our family tree over the last few years he asked me if I would write to you.

We have good facilities in Bradford for tracing our ancestors, the whole of the sixth floor of the Central Library being given over to genealogy. I have used the facilities on and off for the last twelve years. Mainly looking at the census reports; many a time drawing blanks and getting rather despondent and losing interest for a year or two.

At the present time I have managed to trace my line back to 1837 - viewing proofs of birth certificates, wedding certificates etc. but have for now reached a blank to further searches.

My ancestors throughout the 1800's worked in the Bradford Mills, man women and children.

The mills that my ancestors worked for in the Bradford area were in the Laisterdike area. The wool trade in this town of Bradford has now completely disappeared, and the image of the city has changed to a cleaner city with a thriving tourist trade. There are lots of different things to offer to the tourists now.

Most of the Bradford mills have been preserved and put to other uses, i.e. Millshops, DIY shops etc. There are also large areas of the old terraced mill houses, which have been stone cleaned and modernised.

To further your studies on the Swaine name in Bradford, I would recommend you to read the book by Cudworth called 'Rambles around Horton' published in 1886'. I read this earlier this year.

Mr Cudworth, who lived in the old area Bradford called Horton describes the formation of Bradford from at least the sixteenth century to the Industrial Revolution, and by whom. A man named Swaine was involved as a partner in the building of the first steam powered mill in Bradford in 1804. It is still there today.

Whilst I always had the impression that the name Swaine was not very common. After reading Cudworth I find things are to the opposite, the name Swaine was very numerous in early Bradford and very influential. Also very rich (but alas, no connection with my branch). The Swaines of the 1700's & 1800's in Bradford had in their possession at one time or another all the large halls, of which some are still standing. They also figured strongly in church life.

In the Cudworth book there is a whole chapter given over to the Swaine name and history including a fold-out family tree of the most influential Swaine line from the 1500's to late 1800's. The Swaine family was spread far and wide including a Colonel Von Swaine in Germany. Cudworth constantly draws one's attention to how well known the Swaines were for their longevity and mentions an Abraham Swaine following the plough at 95 years of age in the 1800'!

Yours sincerely,
Louis Swaine

Irish Connection

Jean Usher, Rangiora, New Zealand.

You recently wrote to my cousin John Swaine of Culverden, and he handed me your letter to answer, as he new I was interested in the subject.

One William Swaine was born in Camolin, County Wexford, Ireland. He came to New Zealand in the 1850's and married a Margaret Fyfe on 30-1-1857. His parent's names were Roger and Cecilia. William had five brothers, one of which, Richard, still has descendants in Wexford.

Alf Swaine, Mid Canterbury, New Zealand.

My father's ancestors came from around Camolin, County Wexford, Ireland.

I was in Ireland in the summer of 1975 visiting a cousin. I asked them where his ancestors came from, and he understood that it was from one of the Scandinavian countries.

5 Southfield Crescent,
Dringhouses,
Yorkshire.

I noticed you state that 'according to Halberts' the origin of the surname Swaine can be associated with the Irish meaning 'descendant of Swain'.

Actually, in the Irish language or Gaelic, it is known as MacSwain, or in English - the son of Swaine. However, on referring to Irish history, the name is supposed to have really originated from Denmark, where it is spelt as Sven.

Towards the end of the 10th, and the beginning of the 11th centuries, the Danes, led by King Sven invaded Ireland, They were, however, eventually defeated by the Irish under the leadership of King Brian

Boru, at the Battle of Clontarf in the year 1014 AD, and driven out of the country.
Of course some of them escaped and settled in England. They obviously intermarried with the natives.

Yours sincerely,
Jim Swaine.

Snippets

James R Swaine - Iowa

My grandfather was Truman Swaine born June 1st 1857 in Buffalo, New York. My great grandfather was James Swaine, born Oct. 18th 1822 in England. My great great grandfather was James Swaine born Oct. 18 1782 in Todcaster, and came to the USA from Yorkshire County sometime between the years 1840 and 1844. I am wondering where you got my name from etc?

Fred Swaine - Winnipeg, Canada.

My father changed his German surname from Schwein to Swaine shortly after the First World War. I am told that it is a faithful translation meaning 'pig herder'. There are no known English relatives. Did you get my name from my son Luke, who is attending the University of Sussex?

John Swaine -

My grandfather was apparently a sailor at Rye, owning a number of fishing boats at one time. His family lived in a cottage, where now there is a cinema. He later moved to Tenterden, after marrying a Miss Curtis.
His father, circa 1818, was Joseph Swaine, reputed to be a smuggler and shot by revenue officers, although not mortally wounded.

Ada Percy (Swaine), Leeds.

It may interest you to know, that I was once told by a friend who was interested in heraldry, that William Pitt's grandmother was called Swaine.

John Swaine, St Albans.

My paternal grandfather was Frank Arthur Swaine, a well-known society photographer and artist, who had a studio in New Bond Street, and was appointed by Royal Command to several European royal families (but not Britain's). His father was Arthur Swain, about whom we know nothing except for his belief that he was related in some way to Captain Cook. I rather think that a link to your lines is unlikely. However, I would be interested to hear if we do indeed join up.

J. Swaine, Southampton.

My late father had a considerable interest in the subject, and I enclose a summary of his findings. As you can see, he has established a link to Monomy Swaine, a marine artist who exhibited at Greenwich and John Evelyn the diarist.
If any of this connects into your research I would be glad to hear.

Catherine Trotman (Grandaughter of Samuel Tovey Rawlings)
Bath

What a terrible stories those gravestones reveal? I can remember my Mother (Lucy Rawlings) telling me they died of tuberculosis. We have made some progress. I believe Jane's family, Rawlings, also had t.b. Her father died fairly young leaving many children, and I can remember my mother telling me her grandmother had a shocking cough 'The Rawlings Cough'.

(Catherine was the daughter of Lucy Sophia Rawlings and Edward Vaughan Trotman of the Frome Brewing family. Catherine, a cousin, was close to the Swaines on The Bridge throughout her life. She never married and died in 1999).

Other Recordings

Dorset Epiphany Sessions 6th Jan 1835 Dorchester

Hannah Swayne, aged 43 of Tyneham, charged with stealing from Grace Mowlam one table cloth, one white petticoat, one black shawl and one white calico apron marked GM.

Hannah Swayne the prisoner in her defence says 'I claim the things. I never stole any thing from any one.

Verdict: Hannah Swayne, guilty - 7 years Transportation.

Somerset Michaelmas Sessions, 13 October 1817, at Taunton

John Parsons, aged 15, labourer of Frome Selwood, Somerset. Charged with stealing a smock frock the property of James Coward.

The said Mary Vigor on her oath saith that this morning about half past ten o'clock as she was passing the shop of the said James Coward she saw John Parsons take from a hook on the outside of the shop door of the said James Coward a new smock frock and carry it away with him.

Verdict: John Parsons, guilty - 7 years Transportation.

SAMUEL RAWLINGS   &   SOPHIE TOVEY
b.1802   (Islington)
Founder of S.Rawlings & Sons
Cardmaker,later Canvas/Leather.
Trading in Frome until 1972.
Production transferred to Yorkshire.

⋮

⋮   ⋮

SAMUEL TOVEY RAWLINGS = EMILY JANE MILLETT JANE
1842-1913   of Beckington   m.
S. Rawlings & Sons   1839-1926   James Treasure
⋮   SWAINE

LUCY SOPHIA b.1868
m.
Edward Vaughan Trotman
d. 1966

⋮   ⋮

DOROTHY V.   CATHERINE
b. 19-6-1896   b. 14-3-1908
Lived, Nunney Road.
Frome

EXTRACT FROM RAWLINGS FAMILY TREE

GEOFF SWAINE

WILLIAM & ELIZABETH TREASURE
b. Bruton. Founder   1811-1895
of Tailoring Business
1812-1889
:
:
:
JAMES TREASURE SWAINE - JANE RAWLINGS
d.1915   d.1941
:
_____:_____
:   :   :   :   :
HELEN FRANCES JAMES FREDERICK THOMAS MARGARET JANET EDITH
:   :   :
:   :   :
m. NEALE   m .ETHEL MAUD   m. A Snashall
             SHELTON   :
:   :
:   Margery
_____:_____
:   :
MARY MILLICENT   WILLIAM HERMAN
b 1910   SHELTON
:   b 1913
:   :
:   :
m. JOHN MATTHEWS   m. REBECCA (Betty) MARTIN
Hereford   London
_____:_____   :
:   :   :   :
SUSAN ANNE JOYCE   :
_____:_____
:   :   :
GILLIAN   GEOFFREY   ANGELA
b 1940   b 1942   b 1945

PART OF THE SWAINE FAMILY TREE

Extracts from various Census & other Records in Frome Library (as recorded)

Census 1841 Frome

Catherine Hill

William Swaine	25	b. Somt.	Tailor
Francis.	4 b.	Somt.	

Catherine Street

Martha Treasure	60	b. Somt.	Independent
James	65	b. Somt.	Cordwainer
Sarah	60		
Sophia	30		
Thomas Bould	25	Grocer	
Ann	35	Dau. of James Treasure	
Elizabeth ..	6		
Jane	3		
Esther Edwards	55	Independent	
Elizabeth Swain	30	Tailoress	
James	1		
Ann Wilcox	16?	F.S.	
Ann Ford	45	Independent	

The above entry is difficult to read in places. F.S. = Female Servant. Ages were supposed to be given to the nearest 5 years after the age of 15. (i.e. 20, 25, 30, 35 etc.)

Burials

In the register of Badcox Lane Baptist Church - Usually in Catherine Hill Burial Ground.

30-11-1685   James Treasure Swaine, aged 19months, son of William Swaine, tailor of Catherine Hill.

30-11-1685   Ann Bould (Husband - Thomas) of Bristol, dau. of James Treasure. Deceased aged 35.

30-11-1685   James Treasure, Shoemaker, Catherine Hill, aged 70.
30-11-1686   Ann Treasure, widow of James, High St. aged 75.
               James Treasure married Ann Budgett, 18th April 1797.

Census 1851 Frome

The Bridge

William Swaine.	Head m.	38	b. Bruton	Tailor Employs 15 men.
Elizabeth	wife	39	b. Frome	
James	son	10	b. Frome	Scholar
Fanny E.	dau.	8	b. Frome	Scholar
Albert T.	son	6	b. Frome	Scholar
Agnes	dau.	4	b. Frome	At home
Emily Ann	dau.	1	b. Frome	
Sarah Treasure	sister in law	u.50	b. Frome	Former house-keeper
Mary Williams		u.18		House servant

Wallbridge House

Elizabeth Swaine	u.29	House maid, servant of John & Elizabeth Sinkins

Keyford Street

Ann Swain	visitor	u. 76	Cloth stainer

1871 6 The Bridge

William Swaine	Head	m.58	Master Tailor
Elizabeth	wife	59	
James Treasure	son	u. 30	Son and partner
Ellen Budgett	dau.	u.16	Scholar
Lydia Grantu.		16	General servant

1881 6 The Bridge

William Swaine   Head   m.68   Tailor. Master, employs 11 men.
Elizabeth   wifem.   69
Agnes S.   dau.   u.34
Ellen B.   dau.   u.26
Pamela Pearceu.   21   Domestic servant

St John's Church, Frome, Baptisms

18th August 1789   John Swaine b. 23-9-1788,
                        son of William and Joanna.
20th August 1803   Ann Swain aged 24 years,
                        dau. of William and Jane, nee Budgett.
2nd May 1811   Elizabeth Treasure aged ?
                        dau. of James and Ann, nee Budgett.

Badcox Lane Baptist Church

Register of birth
William Francis,   b. 21-8-1836,   son of William and Elizabeth Swaine.

Vaccination Register Aug.1853 - Dec.1858

Ellen Budgett Swaine,   Bridge.   Dau. of William, Master Tailor.

St John's Church, Frome. Marriages

30-11-1685   William Swain and Joan Button
April 1792   Ann Swain and James Hunter
25-5-1795   Joseph Swaine & Mary Snelgrove. Both of this Parish.
24-2-1802   Samuel Swaine & Ann Pobjoy. Both of this Parish.
11-4-1803   Mary Swain & Benjamin Wilkins. Both of this Parish.
5-10-1807   Joannah Swayne & Henry Hedges. Both of this Parish.
15-2-1808   John Swayne & Elizabeth Budd. Both of this Parish.
30-11-1685   Ann Swain and Charles Dunn
30-11-1686   Thomas Swain and Ann Hoskins
(The above entry shows how the name can easily become varied).

Voters Lists 1834, Frome & District

Abode	Qualifications	Place or Tenant
Samuel	Keyford	Freehold house Self

Listed 1834 to 1847 Entry crossed out and marked 'objected'

(shame about him)

Bath & Wells Diocese Marriage Licence Bonds

Date of Bond

30-11-1685   Jane Swain, widow over 21 and Thomas Pike. Wdr.

30-11-1686

Both of Road, to marry at Road. Bondsman - W Pike
(The village of Road later became Rode, and it has two churches, each carrying one of the spellings of the name).

30-11-1685   Thomas Swain Junior & Rose Cleaves both of Doulting.

30-11-1686   Elizabeth Swain, sp, over 40 & Henry Phelps, over 60.
Both of and to marry at Brewton (i.e. Bruton).

30-11-1685   Ann Swaine, sp, minor & Charles Dunne, tailor.
Both of Frome.

30-11-1685   Christian Swayne & James Pointing, both of Bruton.

30-11-1686   Thomas Swain, tailor & Ann Hoskins, both of Frome.

Pre 1755 Male Entries only, all of the diocese.

30-11-1685   Walter Swayne of Mere & Ann Cheart of Quantoxhead at Wells Cathedral.

30-11-1685   Henry Swayne of Hilperton, Wilts. Clockmaker, & Mary Tily of Laverton.

30-11-1685   Robert Swaine, Winscombe & Sarah Neighbours.

30-11-1686   Stephen Swaine (signed Swayne) of East Brent & Elizabeth Wride of Lympsham.

Wells Cathedral Marriages

30-11-1685 Walter Swaine, Meare & Ann Shirt, Quantoxhead.
(Some above entries show contradiction of names. Particularly noticeable is the naming of Ann Shirt, where just above it is written as

Ann Cheart. An obvious example of a registrar or clergyman writing down the name just as he heard it. No wonder the spellings got changed over the years).

Gravestone
The gravestone in the Vallis Way Nonconformist Cemetery at Frome shows that William and Elizabeth, (founders of the tailoring business), had eight children, six of which died at a young age. A letter from Catherine Trotman reveals that TB was the scourge. Only James Treasure and Sarah Bessie survived into old age.

Inscription Reads
In affectionate Remembrance of the beloved children of
William and Elizabeth Swaine
Fanny - who died August 16 1836 aged 2 years.
James Treasure - who died August 25 1840 aged 1 year 8 months.
William Francis - who died June 4 1849, aged 15 years.
Interred at Catherine Hill Burying Ground (The above)
Also of (Interred at this grave)
Emily Anne who died July 20 1860 aged 11 years.
Albert Tom who died March 5 1864 aged 19 years.
Frances Elizabeth who died May 19 1869 aged 26 years.
Also of the above
William Swaine who died Dec. 23 1889 aged 77 years. (1812-1889)
Elizabeth his wife who died March 31 1895 aged 84 years. (1812-1895)
Also of
Sarah Bessie Swaine. Daughter of the above who died August 6 1914 aged 62 years.
The gravestone had additions constantly added to it and became full, as did the grave. We know that there is another grave close by, but it was only from Mrs Massey's records that we could locate it and obtain the inscription.
In loving memory of James Treasure Swaine born Nov 2 1840, died Nov. 8 1915, and Helen Francis Neale 26 Dec. 1871 - Sept. 18 1961. Also of Charles Edward Swaine, born Oct. 15 1877, died June 3 1878, and Jane Swaine died July 7 1941 aged 97 years.

Letter to Local Paper

Who knows about this shed?

ON a recent visit to Frome I was having a look at the railway station when I noticed the old railway shed now used by SDS Limited.

I believe this shed to be from the early broad gauge days of the Great Western Railway. Also it may well have been a transfer shed where goods were transferred from broad gauge to standard gauge. This would be similar to the one that has been restored at the Didcot Railway Centre.

The arch which shows in the photograph (above) is undoubtedly to suit broad gauge stock.

In Mr Goodall's excellent book on The Buildings Of Frome, the station history is well noted, but not the shed. I would be grateful if somebody could send me some details of this shed.

GEOFFREY M H SWAINE
59 Stanley Road
Clacton-on-Sea
Essex

PS — I am a descendant of W Swaine and Son, tailors of The Bridge, Frome, 1837-1935.

170

Around the Station

Letter to the Editor

Somerset Standard 15th September 1989

On a recent visit to Frome, I was very pleased to see how well kept the town is, as I spent much of my childhood there.

I was especially pleased that the town railway station has been repaired, and is assured of preservation.

On my recent travels, I visited the Great Western steam centre at Didcot. I noticed that the Frome North signal box has been preserved there, together with the main signal box at Radstock.

A section of track has been set up between both of these signal boxes, and will soon become a functional example of single track working.

Steam trains will pass from one signal box to the other with full signalling, etc.

I wonder what became of the main Frome signal box. I would be grateful for a photo of this if anybody has one.

G.M.H. Swaine

A Price - Frome
(Extract from letter dated Jan. 1993)

The station, which is a Grade 1 listed building, and the goods shed, which is not, scream 'Brunel'. However, it is unlikely that the great man himself had much to do with them, as by 1850 he was involved in other far more 'high profile' projects. Both buildings were built in the 1850's, and has been generally attributed to J.R. Hannaford, a Brunel disciple and employee.

In the 1900's there were some thirty horses working from Frome and a similar number of vans, drays and carts. The beasts were stabled near the goods depot until about 1926 when a new stable was built on the south side of the main line.

The 30's must have seen the heyday of Frome as a railway goods depot. The main outgoings would have been rural produce and that mainly associated with the dairy industry and the thriving market in the town. Additionally there would have been brewery products, printed materials, non-ferrous castings pressings and machinings. Not forgetting imported merchandise, and by the 1960's all this would have been taken by motor vehicles. The goods facilities at Frome were withdrawn in 1966.

Sadly, the future of the goods shed structure is now very uncertain. I will be very surprised if it is still there in 5 years time as the whole area is ripe for redevelopment.

M Poole - Frome.

I was very interested in your photograph of the old Clink railway bridge, and also the signal. I was going to take a photo of it myself before it was all taken down, and the by pass bridge was put in its place. I was in the signal gang that erected it, and so I was delighted with the photo.

I was in the Signal and Telegraph Department at Frome in 1950.

WELSHMILL

FORMER MILL

BRANCH LINE

WELSHMILL ROAD

N

FROME FIELD

To Clink →

WEST END

garden

MARKET HALL

TRINITY AREA

CONVENT

CONIGRE HOUSE

SINGERS FACTORY

CATTLE MARKET

BRIDGE ST

NORTH PARADE

CORK STREET

MARKET PL. THE BRIDGE

BLUE HOUSE

WILLOW VALE

RIVER FROME

CATHERINE HILL

STONY ST.

CHEAP ST

KING ST

CATHERINE HILL HOUSE

SHEPPARDS BARTON

SILK & CREPE FACTORY

FIRE STATION

CHRISTCHURCH ST W.

ROOK LANE CHAPEL

BATH STREET

GENTLE ST.

ST. JOHN'S CHURCH

KEYFORD

PORTWAY
To Station →

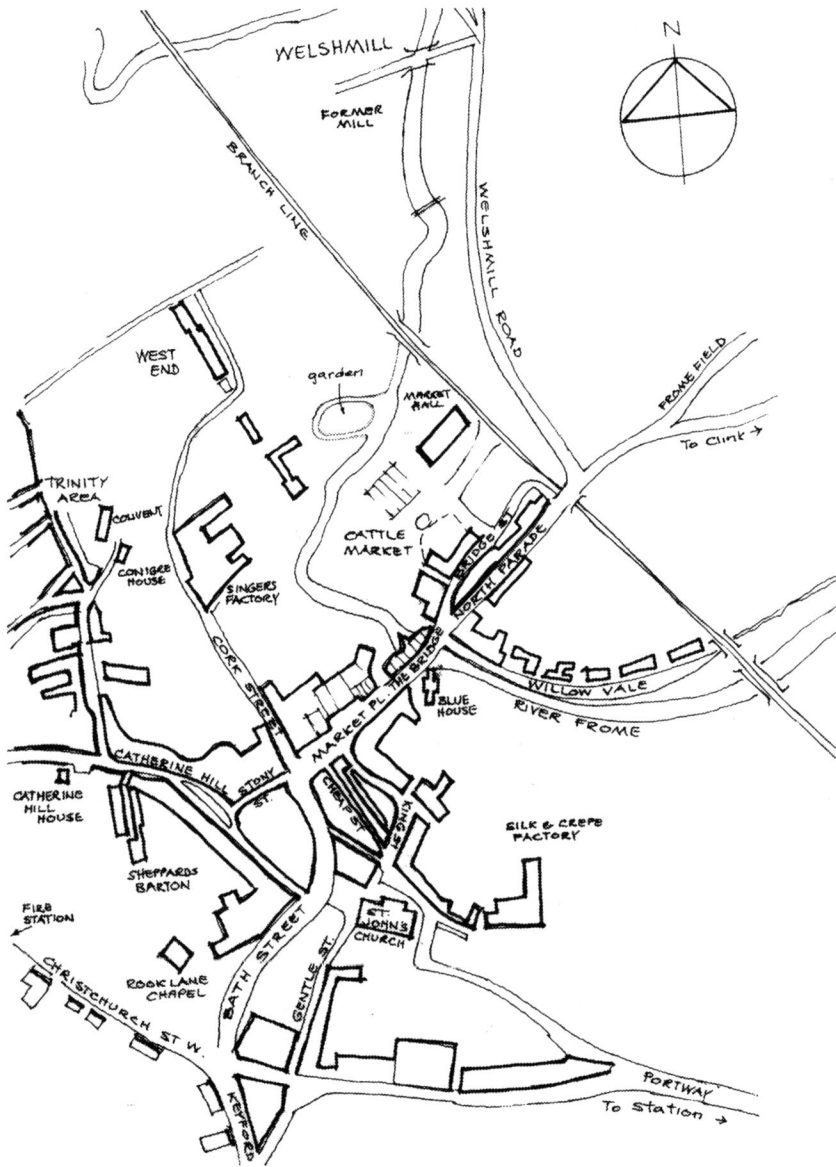

Frome Town Centre - 1920

173

A visit to Evercreech in 1993 with my father was for the occasion of the 80th birthday celebration of his cousin Irene, (his mother's family). The family kindly gave us a wealth of new and forgotten family information. One item, which was a real find for the album, was the courting photograph of my grandfather and grandmother on the river at Frome.

Anatomy of a photograph

Frederick and Ethel, obviously in their courting days. As they were married in 1907, the photo dates before this.

It was taken at Welshmill, down-river from The Bridge.

The little suspension bridge is no longer there, but I do remember it in the 1950's.

After they married they set up home just north of this point at No. 9 West End.

Certainly this would have been a posed photograph. Frederick would have shown much displeasure at an intrusion.

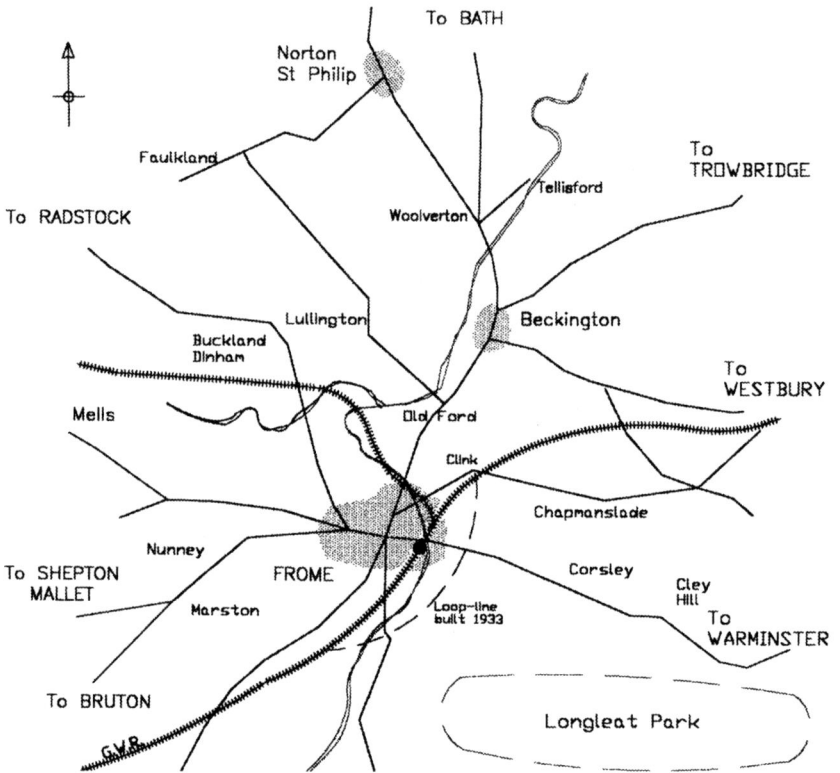

The Environs of Frome - 1910

176

Life Structure of the 1800's.

Catherine Street is on the edge of the Trinity housing and was built as part of that estate. With extensive workshops on the east side, their original facility was to serve the cloth industry. The workshops fronting onto the street had the ability to do trading with the public. Gradually this retailing side grew until they became fully-fledged shops from about the 1800's.

Catherine Street led into Catherine Hill where William Swaine had his home and business, and it was in Catherine Street that his wife Elizabeth, had formerly lived. Her father was a shoemaker, and the census of 1841 attributed 12 people to their household. William and Elizabeth married at St Johns in 1834, and they were to have 11 children. Only 4 of those survived past the age of 26 with the first three all perishing before 1840.

Revolutions in Services after 1840

Formal Records began for births, marriages and deaths.
Gas available for Light and Heat
The coming of the Railway
Introduction of the Local Paper
Piped Water
Mains Sewage Disposal
Invention of the Motor Car
Introduction of Electricity

Although the town was mostly in depressed times during this period, due to the contracting of the cloth industry. It can be seen from the above introductions that the Victorian times were extremely progressive.

As time has gone on since the Industrial Revolution began in the century before, the speed of progress had got faster and faster. The progress made in the 1900's seems to have outstripped all the progress made previously since pre-historic days.

The daily life of those working in a tailoring shop, or any other inhabitant of the town, would have had their lives enhanced by the introduction of any one of these new modern services, during the later part of the 1800's.

Gas lighting took the gloom out of a winter's night and effectively extended the hours in an evening, before going to bed. Streets became less gloomy and slowly encouraged people to travel about after dark.

With gas cooking and with main sewers being introduced, hygiene around the home improved dramatically. All this gave better prospects for child survival, and as we have seen in the Swaine family many children who had not survived infancy.

The child mortality which hit the family was in fact very typical of nearly every family across the country. To look through the parish records of any town the picture is the same. A child born in Victorian times had more chance of death than survival.

At the time of birth, many families thought better than pay half-a-crown for the services of a mid-wife. In their place a 'knowledgeable' aunt may manage the birth proceedings, and many bad practices would thus be incurred. The conditions were mostly so bad that the infant did not have much of a chance of getting past life's first hurdle.

Any complication was nearly always fatal, and not only for the child, often for the mother as well. Whether at birth or in infancy the odds were stacked against a child's survival.

The typical housewife would very likely become pregnant in every year of her active married life and it is not unheard of for a woman to have had as many as eighteen children. How many of those that survived is another matter.

In the early years most children suffered from malnutrition and with hygiene standards so low, infants and young children were not able to show resistance against the many diseases, which were rife.

From the age of 12 a child was considered to be an adult and was expected to work full time. This may have been up to 14 hours a day and of course work may not have been a new experience for these 12-year-olds. Most would have been working in some capacity before this.

Schooling was not compulsory for most periods of the 1800's, but children were expected to attend certain classes. Those who did not attend regularly were those who were kept back by their parents so that they could work. Others may be dim kids who were considered imbeciles (many damaged at birth). They had to join with the unwanted illegitimate children to inhabit the workhouses.

With so much child mortality about during those times, it is sometimes difficult to trace accurately a family tree. There was a habit amongst families to give a first-born son the favourite family name. But if that child does not survive very long, that same Christian name would then be given to another son who came along afterwards. Hence, this can make some of the tracing back into the records a rather treacherous procedure. If the recording of a birth does not correspond with the exact age at death, then this duplication might well have happened.

With the coming of the railways the tailoring shop would suddenly have been able to expand its range dramatically. Soon they could stock Tweeds from Scotland, patterned cloth from Yorkshire, latest linens from London, and not forgetting the fine black cloth, which was still available locally from the Sheppard Mill. Soon my great grandfather would be advertising - London Fashions Regularly Received, and later to be followed by 'The Newest Materials and Latest Paris and London Fashions are Received Monthly.'

The railways also enabled people to be able to travel to the coast for the first time. Brunel's broad gauge railway ran directly to Weymouth passing through Frome, and families used this facility with great relish. More ambitious travellers may take the train to London. Many witnessed the greatest exhibition ever. The 1851 Great Exhibition of world goods in Hyde Park.

All these advances helped Frome to re-establish itself after the decline of the cloth industry. New trades used all the facilities available. Goods and materials were delivered, firstly to the Station Goods Yard, and then by the Railway's horses and carts right to the door. The railway was the 'common carrier' and was obliged to carry and deliver anything that anybody wanted. Many industries expanded during this time including, Brewing, Printing, Building, Newspapers, and especially Shops.

This ability to deliver enabled W Swaine to expand the premises in the 1870's, and by 1881 he was, according to the Census of that year, employing 11 men. Obviously both men and women took the chance to buy or have made a range of clothes that was not available to previous generations; it was the day of the Masher (snappily dressed person).

With great improvements in hygiene due to piped water and mains sewers, child mortality dropped dramatically. Nowhere was this more appreciated than in the Swaine family. The absence of these services had attributed to William and Elizabeth losing five children below the age of nineteen.

With the invention of the motorcar in 1886, it was to be a few years yet before it made an impact into people's lives. The great explosion in motor traffic began slowly at the turn of the century, and by 1910 it had taken hold. At last road building and road improvements could be a priority. In the previous seventy years the former Turnpike roads had been neglected with the clamour of people rushing to use the railways. The first three decades of the new century provided the road builders the opportunity to build a network of metalled roads. In the twenties bus services joined all the towns and villages to make communications really easy, and we were into the modern era. Buses could link with the railways and it was soon to be the heyday of the public transport system.

Acknowledgements

Much pleasure and information was derived from the excellent books by Messrs Belham, McGarvie, Goodall and Gill.

I would also like to thank Mrs H Massey for her work in connection with the saving and recording of family records, and supplying me with such useful information.

Thanks also to those kind people who answered my letters. Also to David Bromwich of Somerset County Council for his information about Local History. And to those who responded to my advertisements, including A Price, M Poole and Reg Jefferies.

Lastly, much thanks to my Aunt Margery (Margaret), who purchased the painting by David Grapes of the back of The Bridge at an exhibition at the Portway Hotel. This was in the early sixties, and in 2000 she gave the picture to me.

Geoffreyswaine@aol.com

See also Amazon.com books.

ISBN 141202933-3